The Semai

A Nonviolent People of Malaya

Field Work Edition

Robert Knox Dentan
State University of New York at Buffalo

WADSWORTH

™

THOMSON LEARNING

Wadsworth/Thomson Learning
10 Davis Drive
Belmont, CA 94002-3098
USA

For information about our products, contact us:
Thomson Learning Academic Resource Center
1-800-423-0563
http://www.wadsworth.com

International Headquarters
Thomson Learning
International Division
290 Harbor Drive, 2nd Floor
Stamford, CT 06902-7477
USA

UK/Europe/Middle East/South Africa

Thomson Learning
Berkshire House
168-173 High Holborn
London WCIV 7AA

Asia
Thomson Learning
60 Albert Street, #15-01
Albert Complex
Singapore 189969

Canada
Nelson Thomson Learning
1120 Birchmount Road
Toronto, Ontario MIK 5G4
Canada
United Kingdom

ISBN 0-534-96885-6

The Adaptable Courseware Program consists of products and additions to existing Wadsworth Group products that are produced from camera-ready copy. Peer review, class testing, and accuracy are primarily the responsibility of the author(s).

CASE STUDIES IN
CULTURAL ANTHROPOLOGY

GENERAL EDITORS

George and Louise Spindler

STANFORD UNIVERSITY

THE SEMAI

A Nonviolent People of Malaya

ABORIGINAL TRIBES
of
THE MALAY PENINSULA

SCALE 1:870,000

(Courtesy the Department of Aborigines, Malaysia)

Leta, Sarah, and Jonathan

Foreword

About the Series

These case studies in cultural anthropology are designed to bring to students, in beginning and intermediate courses in the social sciences, insights into the richness and complexity of human life as it is lived in different ways and in different places. They are written by men and women who have lived in the societies they write about and who are professionally trained as observers and interpreters of human behavior. The authors are also teachers, and in writing their books they have kept the students who will read them foremost in their minds. It is our belief that when an understanding of ways of life very different from one's own is gained, abstractions and generalizations about social structure, cultural values, subsistence techniques, and the other universal categories of human social behavior become meaningful.

About the Author

Robert Knox Dentan is associate professor of anthropology and the American Studies Program at State University of New York at Buffalo. Prior to this, he was on the faculty at Ohio State University. He received his bachelor of arts magna cum laude from Yale University, as well as his Ph.D. He has done fieldwork in Malaya and some cross-cultural research at the Human Relations Area Files in New Haven. Dr. Dentan is the author of a number of studies dealing with mental abberration and with cultural ecology. He says of himself: "My main hobbies are listening to romantic and popular American folk music; reading science fiction and detective stories; and going to 'class B' movies. Most of these might be summed up as a generalized hobby: trying to understand why Americans act like Americans. It is for this reason that my appointment at Buffalo is a 'joint' one, in both anthropology and American Studies."

About the Book

The Senoi Semai are of special significance to anthropologists since they, together with the Semang, may represent remnants of a very widespread and ancient population of Southeast Asia that was pushed into the hinterland areas they now occupy by the coming of technologically more powerful people. Quite apart from this special status, the Semai are of interest to us because they are good examples of the semisedentary horticulturalists in forested areas who cut, burn, plant, harvest for a year or two and then move on. This type of subsistence technique has played a very important role in man's development and is still widely practiced in hinterland areas today. But most particularly, the Semai are of compelling and immediate interest because of their nonviolent orientation—a point of view which is projected into many different sectors of their culture.

Robert Dentan brings the Semai world view to the reader in simple, direct language. He describes how violence terrifies the Semai, how they meet force with flight, how interpersonal and marital relationships, sex, and aggression are influenced by the nonviolent image the Semai hold of themselves. But he takes us further, showing us how they conceive of life, death, pain, and the diagnosis and treatment of disease, and how differently these matters are arranged in the Semai system of perception and thought than in the Euro-American system.

Other features of this case study include a detailed look at the Semai subsistence procedures—the preparation of fields, planting, and harvesting; an analysis of the meaning of kinship in the sectors of social relationships, housing arrangements, perceptions of others, and socioeconomic obligations; and a continuing comparison of the east and west Semai, particularly useful because the more sedentary west Semai, in daily contact with the Malays and Chinese, serve as a prediction of the adjustment probably lying ahead for the hinterland east Semai.

But most notably this case study brings to the reader a Semai view of the world and some of the significant things within it. The author achieves this partly through the objectivity afforded by the intellectual discipline of his science. His analysis is sophisticated, and he uses appropriate anthropological concepts for the ordering of his observations. But his penetration of the Semai view is made possible because he and his wife lived with the Semai as much like Semai as the special circumstances of the Western anthropologist would permit. Participant observation of this kind, coupled with the objective methods of science, are in the best tradition of the methods of anthropology.

Fieldwork Edition

At the end of this case study, as Chapter 12, we have included "Living and Working with the Semai," published originally in *Being an Anthropologist: Fieldwork in Eleven Cultures,* edited by G. Spindler. Including this chapter on how Robert Dentan and his first wife, Ruth, did fieldwork among the Semai with the case study will enable students to better understand what stands behind the descriptions and interpretations of behavior in the study itself. Anthropological fieldwork is not only a scientific endeavor, it is an intensely personal experience.

In "Living and Working with the Semai," one gets a vivid impression of the personal meaning of fieldwork, even though the author heeds the scientific objectives and methods of study. The objectives of his research, the methods and equipment used, the problems of survival in an unhealthful location are discussed in such a way that they are treated both objectively and personally at the same time. The Dentans experienced severe physical privation and threat. Living in a totally alien world, they were beset by insects, a rain forest climate, and general discomfort. They were made ill by debilitating tropical diseases. But they acquired friends and experienced the satisfaction of being accepted, nearly as one of them, by the people they came to observe, and they had motivating them the drive to acquire new knowledge and insight into how the Semai lived and the mental organization behind their behavior. It is a strong tribute to the values of anthropology that they came away from their fieldwork experience with the desire to return not only to unanswered questions but to see the people once more. Robert Dentan feels for the Semai and their country "the bittersweet blend of nostalgia and homesickness the Semai call rəniag."

GEORGE AND LOUISE SPINDLER
General Editors

Calistoga, California
1978

Acknowledgments

The absolutely perfect anthropologist would be a modern Renaissance man, an expert in all fields that pertain to human beings. Probably no anthropologist would claim such perfection. The result is that in doing fieldwork an anthropologist incurs obligations to a great many people who aid him in understanding some aspect of the society he is studying. I can acknowledge only a few of these obligations here.

My wife and I received much help and advice from members of the Department of Aborigines of Malaysia particularly from I. Y. Carey, J. M. Bolton, and Inche' Ruslan bin Abdullah. We are also indebted to Lord Medway, Dr. Ivan Polunin, the faculty of the Zoology Department of the University of Malaya, the staff of the Singapore Botanical Gardens, and the staff of the Institute of Medical Research for helping us solve problems of identification and for providing us with hospitality and intellectual stimulation. Our greatest debt, of course, is to the Semai themselves and especially to those individuals who willingly answered long lists of what must often have seemed to be silly and boring questions. I will defer to their wishes and not mention their names, but whatever is worthwhile in this book is mostly the product of their patience and tolerance.

G. P. Murdock, Harold Conklin, Alexander Alland, T. R. Williams, Harold Scheffler, G. N. Appell, and Edwin Hall read portions of this book and made many helpful suggestions.

Finally, the Field Museum of Natural History and M. Louis Carrard kindly supplied me with many photographs of the Semai taken in the early part of this century.

Pronunciation Guide

As Semai concepts differ from Euro-American concepts, so the sounds used in speaking Semai are different from the sounds used in English. What follows is therefore merely a rough-and-ready guide to pronouncing Semai words.

Stress in Semai is on the last syllable of a word, except in the case of words recently taken over from Malay. This stress is especially pronounced in the eastern dialects, but weaker in the west. Typically, the last syllable is pronounced on a slightly higher pitch. This change of pitch is especially noticeable among infants just learning to talk. Semai words are sometimes distinguished from one another by vowel length, a characteristic not found in English. I have indicated vowel length by doubling the letter in the case of long vowels. The "a" sound in mɜnhaar ("generous") is thus longer than that in mɜnhar ("meat"). The English vowel sounds that approximate those used in Semai are as follows:

a, as in f*a*ther
e, as in b*e*t
i, as in s*ee*k
o, as in r*o*pe, but a little shorter
u, as oo in b*oo*t, but a little shorter
ɔ, as ou in *ou*ght
ɜə, as u in p*u*t
ə, shorter than ɜə; slurred over in unstressed syllables (for example, *sɜlai* may be pronounced like sly)

Most consonants have approximately the same value as in English:

j, as dg in e*dg*e
r, trilled as in German
s, midway between s and sh
', a glottal stop, as in Brooklynese "li'l" for little
ch, as tch in e*tch*

The east Semai sometimes nasalize final consonants, that is, consonants that occur at the end of a word. Thus, final -g sounds like -gn, -b like -bm, -d like -dn and -' like -'n. The vowel preceding final -nd or -nh is nasalized.

A final grammatical note: Semai is characterized by the use of infixes, particles inserted into the middle of a word to change its meaning. For example, sɜngɔh might be translated "to be afraid"; sɜrɜngɔh with the infix -ɜr- "to make afraid"; and sɜnngɔh with the infix -n- (sometimes -ɜn-) "a fear."

Contents

Introduction

Identification

THIS BOOK is a short general introduction to the Senoi Semai, a people who live in or near the hills and mountains of central Malaya. The word *sən'oi* means "person." Ethnologists use it to refer to those Malayan aborigines who do some farming and who speak a Senoi language. The Senoi languages belong to the great Austro-Asiatic language family, which also includes Cambodian, the Mon language of Burma, and the languages spoken by some Vietnamese hill people. But Senoi and the closely related Semang languages differ in many ways from the other Austro-Asiatic languages, which linguists usually group together as Mon-Khmer. This fact seems to indicate that the Senoi and Semang have been isolated for a long time from other Austro-Asiatic speaking people. Now the Senoi and Semang are completely surrounded by people who speak languages that seem unrelated to Austro-Asiatic.

The word Semai refers to the aggregate of people who speak dialects of the Semai language. This term is of uncertain origin. Many Semai refer to themselves by other words, like *sən'oi hii'* ("our people"), *mai darat* or *mai səra'* (both terms meaning "they of the hinterlands"). Sometimes in self-deprecation a Semai will use the insulting Malay word "Sakai" when talking about how backward his people are in comparison with the other peoples of the Malayan peninsula. "Sakai" means something like "bestial aborigine" or "slave." On the lips of a non-Semai the term is offensive.

The Semai in any particular area take their group name from that area. For example, there are *mai chənan* ("they of the mountains"), *mai kuui teio* ("they at the heads of the waters," that is, up-river people) and *mai barəh* ("they of the low-lands," that is, people living near the Malay and Chinese towns that are found only in the lowlands).

1

Historical Sketch

The Semai seem to know little about their own history beyond the fact that they were the original inhabitants of the Malay Peninsula. Some Semai say that the Senoi peoples originated at a place called Sakai Jadi (Malay for "Become Senoi") in what is now the western part of Semai-land. Since then, the Semai say, they have always been where they are today. The obscurity of this history is distressing, because many people who have tried to reconstruct the prehistory of Malaya and of southeast Asia as a whole feel that understanding how the Senoi came to be where they are is a crucial problem.

Ethnologists have traditionally divided the Malayan aborigines into three major categories (see map p. ii); the nomadic hunters and gatherers collectively called Semang (including the Kensiu, Jahai, Lanoh, Mendriq, Temoq, Bateq, Kintaq, Pangan, Semaq, Semang, and Semoq Beri); the agricultural Senoi (Semai, Temiar, Jah Hut, Siwang, Mah Meri, and Semelai); and the "Aboriginal Malays" (Belandas, Temuan, Jakun, and Kanaq).

The Semang and Senoi are supposed to represent remnants of once much more widespread populations that have elsewhere been swamped by an immigration of more powerful peoples. As already noted, the Senoi-Semang languages are not related to those of the technologically more developed peoples of Malaya but rather to languages spoken by peoples scattered through Burma and Indochina. Physical anthropologists say that among the Senoi there are traces of a "racial type" whose closest affinities are found among the aborigines of Ceylon and Australia. At any rate, anthropologists have always been intrigued by the possibility that studying the Semang and Senoi might give us some knowledge of how people lived in Malaya and perhaps throughout Southeast Asia before the arrival of the now dominant peoples.

The nonaboriginal people with whom the Malayan aborigines have the most contact are the Malays. Although nothing is known of the initial contacts between the two peoples, the aborigines were eventually forced to give up their lands and to retreat into the hills in the face of Malay technological superiority. Conceivably a series of defeats at the hands of the Malays led the aborigines to adopt a policy of fleeing rather than fighting, and this policy may in turn have encouraged the development of the emphasis on nonviolence that characterizes present-day aboriginal society.[1] The conversion of the Malays to Islam, beginning some time in the fourteenth century A.D., may have exacerbated the relations between Malays and aborigines. To an ordinary Malay of that period, aborigines probably seemed to be not merely cultural inferiors but despicable pagans to boot, "Sakai" good for nothing but slaves. Malay slave raids on Semai settlements did not completely cease until the beginning of the twentieth century.

Although relations between Malays and aborigines are peaceful nowadays, the general Semai attitude towards Malays remains very ambivalent. On the one

---

[1] P. M. Gardner offers an intriguing theory of "Semai-type" societies in "Symmetric respect and memorate knowledge: The structure and ecology of individualist culture," *Southwestern Journal of Anthropology* 22 (1966):389–415; but he seems to feel his description relevant only to nonagriculturalists.

hand, people are very suspicious of Malay intentions towards them. On the other hand, they admire the superior technology and "wisdom" of the Malays. A Semai usually talks about Malays as if a Malay were the exact opposite of a Semai, a sort of ultimate "other" against which he can assess and measure his own people. Even when talking about how Semai live and act, people constantly contrast themselves with the Malays, for example, "We don't know anything about religion; Malays are always talking about religion."

During the early 1950s there was a Communist uprising in Malaya. As the only people occupying the hills where the guerrillas took refuge, the aborigines willy nilly held a position of tactical importance to both sides. The British, then colonial rulers of Malaya, first tried to relocate the aborigines in camps outside the rain forest. The death rate in these camps was so high that some Semai still regard their relocation as the first step in a campaign to exterminate the aborigines. Later on, the British settled the aborigines around strategically located "Jungle Forts" from which their activities could be supervised. Their stay in the world outside the rain forest reinforced Semai opinions about the viciousness of non-Semai. It also gave people from the more isolated areas their first chance to acquire such non-Semai valuables as wrist watches and pretty woven cloth. This period also saw the formation of a Malayan Department of Aborigines charged with looking after the welfare of the aborigines, a task which today it is performing ably.

The "west Semai" mentioned in this book are much more in contact with the Malays than are the people I call the "east Semai." By constantly comparing these two groups I have tried to give some idea of the changes the history sketched above has effected in Semai society. Although the west Semai strongly resist being swallowed up in Malay society, they have nevertheless become in some ways very much like Malays. Similarly, a large element of the east Semai population seems to consist of Semang who have settled down without altogether giving up their traditional ways of living and thinking. This pattern of change within Semai society may be representative of a general pattern of change throughout Malaya. It seems possible that the three categories of Malayan aborigines are not watertight; that the Semang have for a long time been settling down and becoming Senoi, and that many of the so-called "Aboriginal Malays" are not Malays unconverted to Islam but Senoi who have become "Malayized" to the point of no longer speaking Senoi. Whether or not there is such a general pattern of change, the contrast between east and west Semai should throw some light on the changes occurring in Semai society.

Other factors increase the differences between the east and west Semai. Each Semai settlement is politically autonomous, free to go pretty much its own way. Furthermore, there is little communication between groups of Semai who are distant from each other. Indeed, to talk just about east and west Semai is an oversimplification. According to the census there are Semai in the Cameron Highlands, in north central Semai-land, whose life is shaped by their work on tea plantations. The southeastern Semai seem to have adopted the political system of their "aboriginal Malay" neighbors. In the northwest there are Moslem Semai, people say, and so on.

These differences pose a serious question. Is it legitimate to write a book called "The Semai" about a people as heterogeneous as this, who do not form a "tribe" in any meaningful sense of the word? Anthropologists first became aware of this sort of problem toward the end of the nineteenth century, but a satisfactory solution remains elusive. The question of just what "ethnic groups" people belong to is especially pressing in Southeast Asia, and the Malayan case is a relatively easy one.

In this book I have tried to solve this problem of "ethnic group identification" or at least to evade it by treating the Semai as a "people" in the sense in which political scientists traditionally have used the word. First, the Semai all live in a definable geographic area. Second, they share a tradition of having been dispossessed and persecuted by non-Semai. Partially as a result, both east and west Semai tend to define their own ways of life as being not only different from but also opposite to non-Semai ways of life. Third, they have a common language which is unintelligible to non-Semai. Finally, they share a common attitude towards a great many things, most notably violence. As a result of these shared factors, they can communicate better, and over a wider range of topics, with each other than they can with non-Semai.

Scope of This Report: Fieldwork

Most of the statements in this book rest on fieldwork done by my wife and myself in 1962–1963. The research was supported by a Foreign Area Training Fellowship from the Ford Foundation and a subsidiary grant from the American Museum of Natural History. We lived in two settlements, one in the northeast part of the State of Pahang and one near the town of Kampar in the State of Perak. Because of their distrust of the non-Semai world, people asked that we not pinpoint the location of these settlements. The approximate location of the first, which has now disbanded, was $4\frac{1}{2}$°N 102°E. The second is at about 4°N and 101°E. My impression is that the first settlement is fairly representative of the Semai living in the northeast part of Semai-land. Similarly, the second seems representative of the westernmost Semai, that is, those living in the Perak lowlands and foothills. The Department of Aborigines kindly let us look at several censuses of Semai-land as a whole. Remarks in this book about the size and stability of settlements and households are drawn from the census of the two areas that the two settlements we lived in seem to represent.

We spent about seven months actually living in each settlement, in addition to a total of about four months spent in hospitals recovering from various diseases acquired in the field. Statements in this book about the "east Semai" rest mainly on data collected in the first settlement and in one across the river which we often visited. The combined population of these two settlements was about one hundred at any given time. Assertions about the "west Semai" are based on data from the second settlement, which included about two hundred people, and on data from two other settlements to which we made extended visits. We talked with a good many more people than these population figures indicate, however, because people were constantly moving in and out of the settlements and because a great many people came from other settlements to see what we were like.

People in general and the Semai in particular tend to act differently in the presence of strangers from the way they usually act. To minimize the effects of our presence we tried to become as Semai-like as possible. We lived in a Semai house, dressed like Semai and joined in various economic and religious activities. Anthropologists call this technique "participant observation." At first, because we are both city people and unathletic, we had trouble doing the simplest things—gathering firewood and water, squatting for long periods, helping clear fields, and so on. Moreover, since the Semai language was unwritten, we had to learn it on the spot in the first settlement. We learned it faster than one learns languages in school, not only because we needed it for our research but also because even anthropologists get lonely when the only way to talk to people is in a language (Malay in this case) that no one involved speaks very well. After about two months we were able to chat fairly freely about ordinary things like gossip, food, and the weather. About the same time my wife's cooking finally came up to Semai standards, and we were both delighted when people praised the taste of a python head she had fried.

Nevertheless, our attempts to become inconspicuous were not altogether successful in the eastern settlement. From the Semai viewpoint we were huge, fantastically rich, and oddly colored. Moreover, since we depended on monthly shipments of food, we could not share our food with the east Semai as totally as they shared theirs with us, for fear of running out. As a result, most of the people never did trust us implicitly, although we did make several friends. For all the affection we gave and received, most of the time it was as if a thin glass wall separated us from the people. For all their mistrust, however, the east Semai never took advantage of us without our acquiescence. On the several occasions when we had to retire from their settlement for hospitalization (once for two months), we left our supplies unguarded in our unlockable house. Although everyone keenly desired the goods we left behind, we never found anything missing on our return.

In the west Semai settlement we spoke nothing but Semai from the outset. Moreover, the west Semai were more familiar with the sight of Europeans, whereas the east Semai had never seen a white woman before. Finally, we could buy most of our food at a local Chinese market, as some of the Semai themselves did, so that we never seemed to be hoarding a huge surplus. The upshot was that our relations with the west Semai were in general more trusting and warm than our relations with the east Semai—there was no "glass wall."

One result of trying to live like Semai was that we gradually found ourselves developing what we took to be Semai attitudes toward a great many things. For example, I remember vividly the unpleasant shock of seeing a photograph of myself with the Semai. Between the time the film had been sent down river to be developed and the time it was sent back, I had, apparently without realizing it, come to think of myself as looking like our neighbors. My wife and I still sometimes respond like Semai in American situations, and we are often seized with homesickness for our Semai friends and their country. Once in a while we still dream in the Semai language.

Our "Semai-ization" is not, however, solely the product of participant observation. P. D. R. Williams-Hunt and H. D. Noone, the only men to do intensive fieldwork with Senoi peoples before us, both took Senoi wives and settled down to live as Senoi. The Semai way of life is remarkably seductive for Euro-Americans. Part of its attractiveness is due to its stress on nonviolence. One reason for reading about the Semai is that, although their technology is so simple that there is no metalwork, weaving, tanning, or pottery, nevertheless they seem to have worked out ways of handling human violence which technologically more "advanced" people might envy.

Aims of This Study

No one can begin to tell the whole story of an alien people. In a book of this length it would be silly even to try. For example, there is no section on "religion" in the following pages. The topic is omitted for three reasons. First, Semai religion includes Malay, Semang, Christian, and Bahai elements, the disentangling of which would require a separate book. Second, partly because of this complexity, no one was able to give us an over-all view of this religion, although everyone knew disjointed "facts." There is a good deal of confusion and disagreement even about these "facts." For instance, most but not all Semai accept the idea that the universe has seven "layers." People cheerfully gave us the names of these layers, but no one could repeat the names in the same order twice. Several times, moreover, people lost count of how many names they had given us and went on to give us eight or nine. Finally, except for a few west Semai mystics, the Semai tend to be unconcerned and skeptical about religious dogma. For example, people describing life after death almost always concluded by saying something like, "That's just a story of the old days. I don't believe it." Instead of dealing with this sort of topic, I have tried to concentrate on those aspects of Semai life which I found especially interesting and which seem to be of special concern to the Semai themselves.

There is one problem all anthropologists face in trying to write about the people with whom they have lived. That is the slipperiness of trying to translate concepts basic to a non-Euro-American way of life into words comprehensible to Euro-Americans. Different peoples cut up their universe in different ways, use different criteria in making choices. There are few words in any language that have precise equivalents in other languages. Take for example a simple pronoun like English "we." There are four Semai words for "we": *jar*, "we-two-but-not you"; *har*, "you-and-me," also sometimes used in the sense of "you-my-good-friend"; *jii'*, "all-of-us-but-not-you"; and *hii'*, "you and us." Translating "you" into Semai would be even more difficult, because the word used depends on the relationship between the people doing the talking. When more complicated concepts are involved, precise translation becomes almost impossible. The closest one can come to an English word like "gratitude," for example, is *səlniil* (roughly, "embarrassment"). This does not mean, of course, that Semai never feel grateful. It means that they categorize their feeling differently. The same difficulty holds for translating complex Semai concepts into English. (It is obviously foolish to think that, because the Semai have a relatively simple technology, they have "simple" thoughts.) For instance, translating *nyani'* as "evil spirit" is convenient, even though *nyani'* are not very spiritual, nor evil in a moral sense. In such cases I have put the translation into quotation marks to stress that the meaning of the English words merely approximates the meaning of the Semai ones. Where an adequate translation would take up too much space, I have used Semai words that I have already defined. Most of these can be found in the glossary at the back of this book.

A note of caution: Writing a book, especially a short general book like this one, an anthropologist must make generalizations and abstractions. Abstractions are extremely useful in coming to grips with an alien culture. Often, for example, using Boolean algebra can clarify an otherwise obscure and alien conceptual scheme. Nevertheless, an anthropologist usually feels that the people themselves have slipped out of his net of generalizations. His friends, the people he lived with for months, have become a featureless mass. The Semai do not all look alike, think alike, act alike, talk alike. Treestump is a clown, Daylight an intellectual, Uproar a schemer, Arecanut a profoundly dissatisfied man. Our adopted father is a deeply thoughtful man, a skillful debater, and a powerful personality. Sterile Mother, perhaps because of her personal tragedy, is the kindest person I have ever met. The thing to remember in reading any ethnography is that the book is about human beings, individuals, who are trying to get along with the cultural means at their disposal, in a world that almost always makes getting along difficult.

The People and Their Country

Population

THE 1965 CENSUS put the Semai population at 12,748, probably a slight underestimate. The Semai are by far the most numerous aborigines in Malaya, making up about a quarter of the entire aboriginal population and almost two-thirds of the agricultural Senoi-speakers. Their numbers seem to be increasing. Since the area of arable land in Semai territory is unknown, realistic population densities are difficult to estimate. It is possible to say, however, that, except where there is population pressure from neighboring Chinese and Malays, population density is far below what Semai agriculture could support. At a guess, population density varies from 5/mi² to 25/mi².

Infant mortality during the first year of life ranges from around 25 percent in the west to over 50 percent in the east. Malaria seems to be the greatest single cause of death in infancy. In the highlands, where malaria is rare, infant mortality is less than on the middle slopes. Somewhat less than 5 percent of the population is sterile. The Semai recognize sterility and call sterile people *manang*.

Male births outnumber female births, as is the case almost everywhere. In most human populations the male mortality rate is also higher, with the result that males do not outnumber females. Among the Semai, however, female mortality is greater than male mortality, perhaps because of mortality after childbirth, with the result that there are more men than women in all age groups.

Race

The Semai are handsome people. Their skin is golden brown, their lips full and occasionally slightly everted. Their hair is glistening black, sometimes with a coppery highlight that probably indicates protein deficiency but may be a "racial" characteristic. Their noses are short and rather broad. Many Semai have slight folds of skin in the corner of their eyes which make their eyes look almond-shaped, al-

East Semai man with "Negrito" features (1962).

though not as slanted as, for example, Chinese eyes. Most Semai have little or no body hair, but a few men in most villages will have heavy body and facial hair.

In the east Semai population, there are some individuals with dark chocolate skins and tightly curled hair, probably the products of marriages between Semai and Semang. Most east Semai men are slightly under 5 feet tall. The west Semai are on the average almost half a foot taller. There are a good many individuals who look like Malays and some who look very Chinese. Between settlements there seems to be a great deal of genetic diversity.

The reason for all this variability seems to be that the Semai often interbreed with people from other ethnic groups: in the east with the Semang and in the west with Malays and Chinese. Chinese traders and ex-guerrillas sometimes settle down in Semai communities and take Semai wives, and there is a good deal of casual sexual contact between traders and Semai women. Although the Semai say that "only stupid, ugly Malays come to live with us," Malay men often get access to west Semai women by wooing, bribing, or threatening them. An occasional Malay man, a misfit in his own society, will settle down with the tolerant Semai. In short, the Semai do not worry about miscegenation, and outsiders often find Semai women both attractive and complaisant.

The Semai, moreover, cannot bear to see children neglected. When a non-Se-

Girl in loincloth (1930s). (Photograph courtesy of Louis Carrard)

mai is in economic distress, the Semai will eagerly agree to adopt his children. During the Japanese occupation of Malaya and the subsequent Communist insurrection, many children "became Semai" this way. The Semai regard these children as true Semai, saying, for example, "His father was Chinese, his mother was Chinese, but he's really one of us."

Any hypothetical "original" Semai stock has been submerged in this welter of interbreeding. The result is that physical anthropologists have long found the Semai an enigma, and the Semai have been classified as almost everything from "Palae-Alpine" to "Australo-Veddoid." The occasional presence of large amounts of body hair, however, does suggest that there is in the Semai ancestry a stock not found elsewhere in southeast Asia.

Health

The west Semai diet is generally satisfactory in terms of protein and caloric intake, although below the nutritional allowances recommended for Malaya. There seems to be some protein deficiency in the East. Almost all the children there have pot bellies due to protein deficiency, worms, malaria, or all three. Goiters due to iodine deficiency are very common among the highlanders in the east.

Chronic pulmonary diseases, endemic in Semai-land, are major killers. Tuberculosis is very common. The worldwide influenza epidemic of 1918 seems to have decimated some Semai settlements. The impact of these and similar pulmonary diseases may be heightened by the fact that east Semai children begin at about the age of two to smoke cigarettes made of home-grown tobacco wrapped in certain kinds of leaves. Nevertheless, an x-ray survey of all Semai failed to turn up a single case of lung cancer.

Because of their closer contact with non-Semai, the west Semai suffer from certain diseases that are rare or absent in the east. For example, the percentage of the population afflicted with whipworm and roundworm is far higher in the west. West Semai groups forced to live downstream from other groups who use the river as a toilet sometimes contract typhoid or paratyphoid from using polluted water. Sexual contact with Malays and Chinese has introduced venereal diseases. Finally, a few Semai have contracted leprosy through their contacts with Chinese lepers.

Malaria probably kills almost as many Semai as pulmonary diseases do, especially on the lower slopes of the mountains where the people live. The people themselves may be partially responsible for the incidence of malaria, because the mosquito that carries the malaria parasite flourishes not in untouched (primary) rain forest but in areas which people have opened up for cultivation. Moreover, since the Semai keep few domesticated animals, the mosquito must rely on humans as its major blood source. Some physical anthropologists believe that the very high incidence of an abnormal hemoglobin (type E) in the blood of the Senoi peoples may confer a partial immunity to malaria.

Epidemic hepatitis, which can almost exterminate a settlement in a month, seems to be the disease the Semai fear most. Yaws is fairly common, as are elephantiasis and other forms of filiariasis. All told, the area in which the Semai live is rather unhealthy.

Of minor complaints the commonest is headache, for which the Semai have a complex taxonomy, and which they say is often due to worry. Colds and runny noses, also very common, are regarded as "children's diseases," like "sniffles" in Euro-American society. Skin diseases affect most of the members of any settlement. Anemia and harelip are also common.

Although the Semai seem generally to be as "intelligent" as any other people, a prolonged high fever sometimes results in a readily identifiable case of mental subnormality. The victim participates as best he can in community activities, for example, pounding grain or winnowing rice. In turn he is dependent on a kinsman who feeds and clothes him, albeit not very well. Unlike Euro-Americans, the Semai do not regard such an unfortunate with horror and disgust.[2]

---

[2] Readers interested in pursuing this topic might read my note on "The response to intellectual impairment among the Semai," *American Journal of Mental Deficiency* 71 (1967): 764–66.

2

Land, Weather, and *Tɜrlaid*

IN THIS and the next two chapters I have taken an aspect of the environment within which the Semai live and tried to show how the Semai respond to it. Sometimes this approach involves splitting up topics ethnographers usually treat under a single heading. For example, Semai housing is adapted both to climate and to the local fauna. House type is therefore discussed both in this chapter and in the chapter on fauna. Moreover, since the Semai respond to their environment the way they conceive of it rather than the way a Euro-American might, it has sometimes been necessary to include topics in chapters that may seem inappropriate. For example, from a Semai viewpoint fungi seem to belong under the heading of fauna, and I have put them there. The justification for this approach, that is, considering certain aspects of Semai culture as environmental adaptations, is that I think they make sense when considered this way while they might seem odd and arbitrary when viewed another way.

It is worth reiterating that an anthropologist's information consists solely of what people say and what they do. When he attempts to give an account of the concepts and attitudes underlying words and acts, he is making inferences. These inferences may well be wrong, warped by his own cultural and personal experiences. The reader might mentally insert "Dentan's impression is that . . ." at the beginning of any sentence that deals with Semai concepts, attitudes, or feelings.

For example, the notion of "natural order" that appears in this and other chapters is not something any Semai has made explicit to me. I think, however, that the Semai do have a feeling that there is a "natural order," that is, a way things should be and usually are. For example, people treat a single death in a settlement as an event which is sad but to be expected in the normal run of life. After two or three deaths in a relatively short period of time, however, people begin to say things like, "It's not *patud*. One death is *patud*. But three? Not *patud*." The word *patud* comes from a Malay word that means something like "fitting, proper, fair, right." The use of this word in the context of natural events suggests that the Semai do feel that there is a way things should be, a natural order, in which deaths occur at relatively long intervals. Similarly, to have two or three of one's children die is expectable and *patud,* implicitly part of the natural order. But to have all one's children die is not *patud.* At any rate, if one assumes that the Semai do have some feeling that there is a natural order, then some of the things they do and say seem more comprehensible than if one does not make the assumption.

Topography

Most of the Semai live in either Perak or Pahang. Perak and Pahang are two States in Malaya, which is the western part of the country of Malaysia and the southeasternmost corner of continental Asia. This marginal position of Malaya relative to the rest of Asia has been used to support the contention that the Semang and Senoi are remnants of a once more widely distributed population. This argument rests on the assumption that, when relatively backward people are found only on the margin of a geographic area, they have been displaced elsewhere in the area by technologically more advanced peoples. This assumption is almost certainly correct in the case of the South African bushmen and may well be correct in other cases, for example, the Tasmanians (marginal to Australia) and the Australian aborigines (marginal to Asia). It is, however, difficult to judge whether it holds for the Senoi and Semang.

Right down the center of Semai-land runs a chain of mountains, the Main Range, about 3000 feet high and 30 to 40 miles wide. Lowland rain-forest blankets this range up to about 2500 feet, with patches of almost impenetrable secondary rain forest where the Semai have abandoned fields that have become infertile. The soil in the mountains is an acidic sandy clay, yellow to red in color. After a heavy rain, this soil becomes as slick as glass. People wearing shoes have to go on all fours to clamber up the steeper slopes. A barefoot Semai, however, stays erect by flexing his toes so that they dig into the slope at each step.

The upper reaches of the major rivers coming down the slopes are very swift and spotted with waterfalls and rapids. After a heavy rain I used to jump into the river at the upper end of the east Semai settlement, swim as hard upstream as I could, and get out of the river at the bottom end of the settlement about a minute later.

Mountains and rivers have had a marked effect on the distribution of the Semai population. The mountainous terrain is so difficult that even expert "jungle bashers" expect to cover less than 5000 yards a day as the crow flies. Semai footpaths, which are often also game tracks, follow the line of least resistance, vanishing into stream beds (where walking is relatively easy) wherever possible. The Semai themselves walk in single file, without spreading out to beat the bush for game as the Semang do. They move at a pace which at first seems deceptively slow to a Euro-American but which they can keep up long after the Euro-American is gasping for breath. The heat, the slippery clay slopes, and the biting insects combine to make walking in the rain forest an unpleasant experience, and the Semai do not take strolls in the rain forest for pleasure.

To go down a large river the Semai use bamboo rafts, probably the best craft for the turbulent rapids and shallows of the rivers. Coming upstream against the current by raft is very difficult, and people usually abandon the raft and return on foot. If rapids and waterfalls are too bad, people prefer not to make the trip.

Because it is easier to travel by river than to clamber over hills, the Semai in a single river basin are more likely to visit each other than to visit people in other river basins. For the same reason, they are very likely to marry people from the same river basin, so that most of the inhabitants of a single river basin tend to be related to each other. The result is that any given river-valley population, being relatively isolated from other Semai, tends to speak its own dialect and to have customs rather different from those of other Semai. Some anthropologists would call this kind of population a "subtribe." Others would say that, because people in a given river valley marry each other much oftener than they marry outsiders, the "subtribe" is more properly called a "deme." The Semai call it a *gu* and say that its members "have the same great-grandparents of great-grandparents." Since the Semai do not trace their ancestry back that far, this saying seems to be a metaphoric way of emphasizing that one feels a kind of kinship with people from one's own river valley. In Perak, in the west, roads now rival rivers as means of travel, and new *gu* seem to be forming along the roads.

This fragmentation of the Semai population means that the Semai do not constitute a tribe or group. West Semai refer to east Semai as "those Semang" or "those Temiar," and the east Semai say that the westerners are "just like Malays." A man from the east, who stresses and nasalizes final consonants, has difficulty understanding a west Semai, who does neither. In short, as already noted, the Semai constitute a people of no political cohesion and considerable cultural and linguistic diversity.

Weather and Adaptation to Climate

Malaya is generally a hot, wet country. Daily temperatures usually range from about 85–95°F. Nights are about 20°F cooler. On the tallest peaks of the Main Range, night temperatures may on rare occasions fall so low as to produce a frost. In the highland parts of Semai country, it rains about two hundred days a year. The wettest months are April and October to November, and the driest are February and July.

Semai houses are almost perfectly adapted to this climate. They are rectangular and raised on piles at least a couple of feet off the ground (see photograph). The piles raise the floor clear of any dampness on the ground and allow a cool draught under the house. The fact that the floors are often made of bamboo slats about an inch apart also permits free circulation of air. If a cooling breeze or rain reduces the outdoor temperature below the indoor one, a Semai may take whatever he is working on outside under the house. He resumes his work there, transforming his house in effect into a two-story structure.

There is often a gap of a foot or so between the walls and the roof, with the result that air circulates freely indoors. The *atap* (see Glossary) roof is steeply pitched, presenting a sharp angle to the sun's rays and allowing a quick run-off of rain water that might otherwise rot the thatch. The gables of the roof extend far enough beyond the walls that neither rain nor direct sunlight enters through the gap

Part of a large east Semai settlement (1962). (Photograph courtesy of Dr. Malcolm Bolton)

between the walls and roof. The dead-air space between the two or more pitches of the roof serves as insulation from the sun. The *atap* itself is made by interweaving the leaves on one side of a palm frond with those on the other side, forming a kind of rectangular shingle. People tie these shingles onto the roof so that they overlap, making a layer thick enough to resist sun and rain. If a few shingles become rotten or are torn off in a storm, it is easy to replace them.

Like housing, traditional Semai clothing was well adapted to a hot, wet climate. At the turn of the century, both men and women wore scanty barkcloth breechclouts or loincloths, those of the men worn so high as to expose the loins and sometimes too narrow to cover their testicles completely. The barkcloth, which the women made by pounding the inner bark of certain trees (notably *Artocarpus* spp.), had a rather loose texture. More extensive clothing was worn mainly on ceremonial occasions. (See photographs.)

Now, in a hot climate two of the most important ways in which the body regulates its internal temperature are radiation and sweating. Traditional Semai clothing maximized the body's ability to radiate heat by maximizing the area of skin exposed. Similarly, sweating could proceed uninhibited by sweat-soaked clothes. The Semai recognize the importance of sweating, saying that a man who sweats heavily has "a good body," that is, is healthy. One reason they give for eating hot peppers and other hot condiments is that such foods make one sweat. The sweaty skin can then be cooled off rapidly by a slight breeze. By exposing most of the skin, aborigi-

Girls in fiber skirts with barkcloth belts (1930s). These skirts are apparently no longer in style. (Photograph courtesy of Louis Carrard)

nal Semai clothing maximized the power of breezes to cool the body. The loose texture of the barkcloth may have had the same effect.

Now the Semai are beginning to adopt Malay or British styles of clothing. There seem to be two main reasons for this tendency. First, according to the Semai, the new clothes are more durable and prettier than barkcloth, although the east Semai still make barkcloth for festive occasions. Second, since contact with non-Semai became relatively frequent, traditional Semai dress has become an object of scorn, ridicule, and contempt. Like most people, the Semai are sensitive to slurs. For example, the east Semai say that they gave up wearing porcupine quills through their noses after the commandant of the camp where they were relocated during the Communist uprising told them, "You look like a herd of water buffalo."

East Semai men now wear cloth loincloths or shorts, often with a tattered shirt as well. The women wear sarongs but leave their breasts bare except when there are Malays around. If she has one, a woman may put on a brightly colored bra ("child's shirt") for a festive occasion or to have her photograph taken. Children go naked, except perhaps for an amulet, until about the age of seven.

Girls in party dress (1930s). (Photograph courtesy of Louis Carrard)

West Semai men wear trousers, shorts, or sarongs and usually European-style shirts. The women dress like Malay women in sarong and long-sleeved blouse, although some of the older women go bare breasted in their own houses. Children over three years old are usually dressed. In short, the social necessities imposed by contact with non-Semai outweigh the advantages of adaptation to the physical environment.

To keep cool the Semai stay out of direct sunlight when they can. They find the idea of sunbathing weird, not only because it involves getting sweaty and uncomfortable but also because, they say, light skin is more attractive than dark skin. This notion of what makes a person pretty reinforces the tendency to stay in the relatively cool shade.

A final way in which the Semai deal with the heat is bathing. Although people know how to make soap from certain plants and will use commercial soap when they can get it, nevertheless they regard bathing primarily as a way of cooling off. People take a dip in the stream after any strenuous activity, men and women bathing separately. The stream near a settlement is divided into three areas: an upstream sector for collecting drinking water, a middle one for bathing, and a downstream one for defecation. Although many Semai, especially in the east, do not bother going to the stream to defecate, no one would defecate in the bathing area.

Semai Meteorology

Apparently the Semai do not think much about the weather. As in most societies, people talk about the weather quite often, but the conversation consists of complaints rather than speculation. Some west Semai have heard that, in the country of the "Pale People" (Euro-Americans), "wind feces" (frost) accumulates to a depth of several feet. A few people find the information mildly interesting, but the common attitude is that it is a matter of little concern to the Semai. In general, the Semai take the onset of the seasons, the heat and humidity, as part of the way the world is, the natural order and not something to speculate about.

The Semai say that some people can dream what the weather will be. Most people, however, are not "adept" (halaa') enough to have such dreams. Besides, although Semai dream theory is very complex, people recognize that the predictive value of dreams is dubious. Semai are therefore hesitant about interpreting their dreams until after the prediction indicated in the dream has come true. Thus no one ever told us about having a weather forecast dream until after the prophesied weather had occurred.

Similarly, the Semai say that in theory it is possible to control the weather. For example, throwing some salt and/or a length of a certain rattan (Calamus ?manau) into a river should bring rain. Techniques of weather control tend to go unused, with the exception of the rituals to drive away thundersqualls, which are discussed below. The only case we heard of in which someone allegedly used a rain-making technique, for example, involved an east Semai man, "Tree," who had just moved out of our settlement after a rather bitter quarrel that involved most of the people in the settlement and also in the settlement across the river. The people who had quarreled with Tree said that he had performed the rain-making ritual shortly after he left, with the result that a heavy rain had raised the level of the rivers so high that people could not get to their fields to finish planting their crops. Tree denied having performed any such ritual and said that people were accusing him only because they did not like him. Tree's "brother-in-law" (mənai), who had rather reluctantly sided with Tree during the dispute, contended that the technique described by Tree's accusers was faulty and could not bring rain. Perhaps, he went on, people were confused by the fact that Tree had recently thrown the sap of a root into the river to poison the fish (see Chapter 3 for this fishing technique). At any rate, he finished, "they tell this story because they need an explanation for why it rained at a bad time, not because it's true."

The reason for giving this exchange in such detail is that Tree and his brother-in-law were probably right in their interpretation of how people were using the idea of rain-making techniques. In other words, the Semai apparently treat this idea not as a blueprint for bringing rain but to bolster the argument for their side in a dispute or to explain an otherwise inexplicable misfortune. The belief serves social ends rather than meteorological ones. Taken out of its social context and treated as if it were an item in Euro-American meteorological science, the Semai notion of how to make rain is absurd. The absurdity, however, lies not in the notion itself but in decontextualizing it.

"Hot Rain," *Nyamp,* and Allied Phenomena

There are three meteorological phenomena that seem to violate the Semai feeling for "natural order": "hot rain," *nyamp,* and thundersqualls. "Hot rain" falls out of a relatively cloudless sky while the sun is still shining. Being caught outdoors in a "hot rain" is likely, people say, to result in fever or jaundice. Some anthropologists would contend that this idea is quite logical: an "unnatural" phenomenon ("hot rain") produces an "unnatural" physical condition (disease). Williams-Hunt (1952:64, 71–72) writes that most Semai amulets are to ward off the effects of "hot rain," but my impression is that most amulets are worn simply to ward off supernatural danger in any form. The current Semai ideas about "hot rain" may be of Malay origin, for, although there are Senoi words for "hot" and "rain," the Semai and Temiar almost always use the Malay phrase *hujan panas* to describe "hot rain."

Nyamp is a fairly rare atmospheric condition that occurs when a downpour stops just at sunset. The rays of the setting sun shining through the moisture-laden air bathe everything in a bright red or yellow light. The sky itself becomes red or yellow. The effect is like being at the bottom of a filthy aquarium and lasts for several minutes. As soon as *nyamp* begins, people rush out and pull their children indoors. All conversation abruptly stops. Within a minute or so, the settlement, normally bustling at this hour, is as still and deserted looking as a drowned village.

The Semai give conflicting accounts of why *nyamp* is so dangerous. Some people say that "evil spirits" (*nyani'*) are abroad, perhaps because the color of the sky "reminds them of our blood." Others say that exposure to *nyamp* causes shooting pains in the side and back, sometimes with fatal results. I think that these explanations represent attempts to rationalize an unease that the Semai feel at this aberration from the meteorological "natural order." It may be worth noting that both my wife and myself found *nyamp* eerie and disturbing.

The red sky at sunset and sunrise is also called *nyamp*. The Semai say that it has the same ill effects as the other form of *nyamp*. On the other hand, perhaps because as a familiar and regularly recurring phenomenon it is part of the "natural order," people do not act nearly as frightened. For example, I found out about the danger of sunset while sitting on my porch with a couple of friends, watching the sun go down. "If you sit around outdoors during *nyamp*, as we're doing now," said one with a smile, "you get sick." "That's right," said the other, "you get sick and die." Neither made any move towards going indoors. My impression is that the only reason sunrise and sunset are said to be dangerous is that, in the Semai language, they are classified under the same term as the more eerie *nyamp*.

Rainbows tend to occur in association with "hot rain" and *nyamp*. Perhaps for this reason they are associated by the Semai with various dangers. Walking under a rainbow, for instance, might cause a fatal fever. Some people explain that when a tiger kills a large creature (for example, pig, man, deer), it flings the victim's blood into the sky. The arc of the victim's blood is the rainbow. Other people say that rainbows form when a "hot rain" sucks the blood from the earth where a tiger has recently made a kill. Rainbows, possibly because of their shape, are also associated with the *naga* or *dangga'*, huge, horned, subterranean dragons. Although the idea of *naga* seems to be of Indian origin, it is widespread in Southeast Asia. There has even been an English expedition to Semelai country to see whether *naga* are really dinosaurs. One old east Semai man, who delighted in "putting me on" (a favorite Semai game), gave a long, dead-pan description of how he had on three occasions (one just a few months before) encountered baby *naga*, "about two feet long." They were too fast and slippery for him to catch, he said, but he drew me a picture of one, horns and all.

Thundersqualls

Thundersqualls seem to be the most frightening violation of the Semai "natural order." The onset is startlingly sudden. The sky turns black, lit by searing flashes of lightning. There is an almost continuous crashing of thunder. Winds reach speeds of 40 or 50 miles per hour in a matter of minutes. The accompanying torrential rain, as much as four inches an hour, poses the danger of flooding even settlements on high ground.

Semai houses, especially the small houses in the east, are not built to take this sort of punishment. They begin to sway, and often a gust of wind will rip off some of the *atap* shingles. The pilings of the longhouses and of the plank houses are usually set deep enough into the soil to withstand the wind. The roof poles, however, are tied on with rattan strips which may be rotten and which tend to fray or come loose as the house sways in the wind. There is also the danger that a tree struck by lightning will smash in the roof. To avoid the danger of being caught under a collapsing roof, people come down from their houses and hurry through the driving rain to take refuge underneath the sturdiest houses in the settlement. Before leaving, they extinguish their cooking fires lest the wind blow the embers into the inflammable bamboo and *atap* interior. Once outside, they build bonfires, partly to keep warm in the sudden chill, partly to keep away wild animals and "evil spirits" (*nyani'*) that ride with a thundersquall.

Mothers cover the heads of their young children to protect them from the sight of the lightning and the sound of the thunder. To older children, the women say "Fear! Fear!" and, covering their own ears to shut out the explosion of the thunder, urge the children to do likewise.

Most thundersqualls, the Semai say, result from human activities. Making too much noise (for example, laughing uproariously), fooling around with dark-colored things (for example, leeches, fire-blackened cooking pots) or playing with flashing things (for example, mirrors, dragonflies) can attract a noisy, dark squall with its flashes of lightning. Breaking the incest taboos, eating mixtures of certain types of food (see Chapter 3), or being cruel to something defenseless may also bring on a thundersquall. In these latter cases, a violation of the social order results in an upheaval in the natural order. Conversely, the prospect of a punitive thundersquall tends to keep people from breaking social rules.

A variety of Semai beliefs keep this prospect in people's minds. The vast number of black and flashing things which one should treat with caution reminds people of the danger of thundersqualls. Moreover, certain rather common plants and animals are associated with thundersqualls. For example, certain kinds of gingerwort must be cooked outdoors for fear of attracting a storm. There is a kind of bird, the common *cheb tadeid,* said to have been "Thunder's" wife when Thunder was a man. A small eyeless snake is referred to as "Thunder's headband." Most important are "Those Beneath the Earth": *naga* and their "adopted children," that is, pythons, crocodiles, and giant monitor lizards. Deep holes in river banks are said to be dwelling places of *naga.* During severe thundersqualls *naga* leave their holes, bringing floods and turning once populous settlements into quagmires.

According to the Semai, the entity chiefly responsible for thundersqualls is Thunder (*Enku*). Whether Thunder is one or many entities is hard to tell, in part because the Semai often do not distinguish between a linguistic category and individuals that belong in that category (see Chapter 3). Asking people how many "Thunders" there are brings frowns of puzzlement. (Of course, asking English-speakers how many phenomena are covered by the word "thunder" might have the same effect.) The question is not one the Semai would normally ask themselves. After thinking the problem over, people usually answer that there must be at least several *Enku,* "because sometimes it thunders in different places at the same time." Occasionally, moreover, people seem to use the word *enku* in as impersonal and abstract a way as the English word "thunder." On the other hand, when no outsider is asking bizarre questions, the Semai usually speak of Thunder as a single, male, huge, black monkey, which rides cumulus clouds (*rahuu'*) together with the less clearly visualized "Wind" and "Rain." For example, one east Semai described Thunder as a gigantic black leaf monkey that makes thunder by throwing coconuts. These coconuts sometimes turn up as "thunderstones" (actually prehistoric stone axes, associated with thunder by people all over Southeast Asia). A west Semai account says that Thunder is like a giant siamang or gibbon, with a bright "red" breast, "as big as King Kong" (the movie about King Kong had recently been shown at a nearby town). Lightning is the flash of Thunder's shotgun, and thunder-stones are his bullets. It would be an error, I think, to take these descriptions too literally. Most Semai seem to enjoy metaphors and are very talented at explaining an unfamiliar set of concepts by referring to a familiar analogous set. The descriptions of Thunder may be at least partially metaphorical.

According to the older anthropological literature, many Senoi and Semang regard Thunder either as a High God much like the Christian God or as the instrument of such a God, *Tak Pedn*. The Semai attitude towards Thunder is illustrated by the following story. *Enku* fell in love with his younger brother's wife, but she wanted no part of him. *Enku* therefore transformed his organ into a sort of Malayan mushroom that looks remarkably like an erect phallus. Unwittingly, the woman sat on the mushroom, slaking *Enku*'s lust. But when the younger brother found out about this trick, he built a fire around the mushroom. And that is how *Enku* (Thunder) got his voice. The narrator of this story usually finishes gasping with laughter. The stories about *Bah Pent* ("Shorty"), the Semai equivalent of *Tak Pedn,* involve even grosser indignities for poor *Pent*. The themes of the stories and the general lack of reverence narrator and audience display make it hard to regard either *Enku* or *Pent* as a High God.

From the Semai viewpoint, stopping a thundersquall involves dealing with Thunder and *naga.* There is a set of rituals for doing so. This ritual complex is more highly developed in the east than in the west, at least nowadays.[1] The following description refers to the east Semai rituals. These rituals are performed by individuals, not by groups. They seem to be spontaneous, except in the case of children, who sometimes need urging.

The most frequently performed ritual is *chəntɔh.* "If we did not *chətɔh,* this whole place would be flat to the ground, covered with mud—and we'd be underneath it." To *chətɔh,* a person holds a bamboo container out in the driving rain until it is nearly full, then with a bamboo knife or machete he gashes his shin, catches his blood in the rain-filled bamboo and flings the liquid into the shrieking wind, crying *"Tərlaid! Tərlaid!* The word *tərlaid* (see also Chapter 6) means roughly "to act in a way that might bring on a natural calamity." The cry is an acknowledgment that one might have committed such an act, for example, have used a mirror outdoors in the sunlight so that it flashed. People disagree about why Thunder and his allies want the blood. Some say the storm creatures eat the blood, others that they paint themselves with blood as, on festive occasions, the Semai ornament their faces and bodies.

Another explanation people offer for *chəntɔh* is that, by punishing themselves for *tərlaid* in this ritual, they assuage the storm creatures' anger and make them pity the frightened Semai. A related way to achieve this end is to tear out a tuft of one's hair, fling it on the ground beneath the downpour and beat it with a heavy pestle, crying *"Adoh! Adoh! Adoh! Adoh!"* *Adoh* is a cry of suffering like "alas" or "ouch." It is noteworthy that in these rituals the Semai are not trying actually to punish themselves but to trick the storm creatures into thinking that the people are actually punishing themselves.

There are other rituals that express overt hostility towards the entities that cause thundersqualls. One involves cursing the squall and Thunder, telling them to go away, preferably to Malay territory. Some west Semai (who the east Semai say are really Malays) were vastly amused to hear a tape recording of an east Semai ordering a thundersquall to move on to their territory. Finally, a man will sometimes rush out with a spear into the blast of wind and rain, stabbing violently into the heart of the storm. The Semai do these things because they are afraid. But their fear is not transformed into reverence or awe towards the hazily defined creatures they say rule the thundersquall.

3

Animals and *Pənali'*

MALAYAN ANIMALS belong to what zoogeographers call the "Malaysian subregion." This area includes Borneo, Malaya, and Indonesia west of Bali. It is what remains of Sundaland, a land mass most of which was submerged beneath about 120 feet of water by the melting of the polar icecaps around the end of the Pleistocene. Several features characterize those parts of Sundaland still above sea level. First, the fauna is varied. There are, for example, at least 129 species of snakes and over 70 species of bats in Malaya. Second, there tend to be relatively few individuals in any species. Mammals especially tend to be solitary or to move about in small groups. The Semai say, for example, that there is never more than one pair of tigers on one hill. Finally, there tends to be a sharp difference between the faunas of the lowlands and those living at altitudes above 3000 feet. Lowland Semai, for example, rarely have a chance to see a serow (the "goat antelope," *Capricornis sumatrensis*) and several informants confused serow with tapir.

The largest Malayan animal is the elephant, which is still common enough in the East to pose a threat to crops. Tapirs are also fairly common, but so shy that the Semai rarely see them. The two almost extinct species of rhinoceros are usually classified by the Semai with tapirs, presumably because the footprints are similar and the live animals rarely seen. Barking deer and wild pigs are important field pests in the east, although they probably do less damage than the numerous species of rats and mice. Tigers, leopards, and a few rather rare other large wild cats are, again in the east, a danger to both the people and their livestock. The bearcat, a civet which weighs 20 to 25 pounds and looks like a wolverine, is said sometimes to attack people. There are several species of smaller civets that often raid Semai chicken roosts. The different kinds of primates include three species of gibbon, three of leaf monkey, two of macaque, and the unique slow loris. Among the odder Malayan mammals are the panggolin or "scaly anteater," the tiny mousedeer and the "flying lemur," which is not a lemur.

Bird life is also very varied. Among the larger and more impressive birds are the argus pheasant, the peacock, and the hornbill. The worst field pests are the munias, weaverfinches, and small birds called "rice-pullers." Birds usually do not make up a significant part of the Semai diet.

Reptiles abound. Malaya boasts the reticulated python, which may be the largest snake in the world. It grows to be 35 feet long and can weigh as much as an eighth of a ton. King cobras, which are up to 18 feet long, are not only by far the world's largest poisonous snakes but also among the most aggressive, sometimes attacking people without provocation. The bite has been known to kill an elephant. The other Malayan cobra is rarely more than 6 feet long, but it can "spit" a fine spray of venom from a range of about 3 feet, usually at the victim's eyes. In the eyes the venom causes great pain, temporary blindness and, if not quickly washed out, permanent damage. There are fifteen other species of poisonous snakes, but only the three kraits are usually deadly to adult human beings. Crocodiles rarely come far enough upstream to be a menace to the Semai. Monitor lizards and pythons form a rather important part of the east Semai diet, although the west Semai will not eat them.

Fish are for the east Semai at least as important a source of animal protein as terrestrial animals are, and in the west fish are usually more important. The most important food fish are carp, snakehead, and catfish, although the Semai eat almost any fish, including some types sold in Euro-American pet stores, like guppies and betas. The Semai say that the giant catfish found in the larger rivers sometimes grows to be 80 feet long and eats people, but this account may be embroidered.

There is a bewildering variety of other animal life. Some species are enormous. One spider, which has a leg spread like a soup plate, eats birds and mice. There is a black scorpion the size of a New England crab but less deadly than some of the much smaller house scorpions that crawl into one's clothes at night. One time I had my pants halfway on before realizing that a mother scorpion and her brood had moved in during the night. Getting the pants back off without disturbing the scorpions is an experience I would not care to repeat. There are several types of venomous centipede over a foot long, as well as small ones that glow in the dark. After a rain the bushes are swarming with small black land leeches that slip through the smallest fold of one's clothing. There are many sorts of insects that bite, but the most annoying insects are the flying ants and the tiny gnatlike *agas agas,* which sometimes swarm so densely around one's lamp in the evening that writing or typing is almost impossible.

The Response to Animals

HOUSING   An east Semai house shelters people against wild animals (especially elephants and tigers) as well as against sun and rain. In the east Semai settlement where we lived there were two kinds of houses. The smaller kind had walls of flattened bamboo and rested on posts that raised it 4 to 10 feet off the ground. It usually held one or two nuclear families.[1] There were also three longhouses, each of which held several related nuclear families. The largest, about 40 feet long, was

---

[1] A "nuclear family" consists of a man, his wife, and his children.

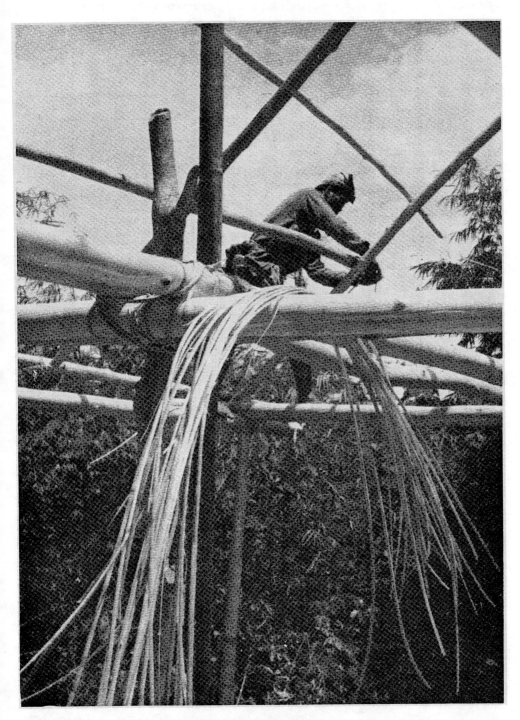

Man building a house.

raised almost 20 feet off the ground. Longhouses are sturdier than the smaller houses. The floors are reinforced, and the walls are sometimes made of bamboo poles rather than flattened bamboo. The smaller houses shudder and sway in a high wind, but the longhouse is relatively steady. Along the walls of a longhouse, each nuclear family has its small sleeping compartment, set off from the others by walls a foot or two high. The central part of the floor, which is usually a foot or two higher than the floors of the sleeping compartments, is reserved for communal activities like cooking or dancing.

When dangerous wild animals like elephants or tigers are around, people from the smaller houses move into the longhouse for the night. For example, one day the women found tiger pug marks at their bathing place. That evening all our neighbors slept in the longhouses. Later that night the tiger came into the settlement and strolled slowly under the houses, probably attracted by the smell of the goats, which had all fled into the rain forest. My wife and I spent several rather tense minutes huddled together on the bed, watching and smelling the tiger, and thinking about how easy it would be for a large animal (tigers weigh up to 750 pounds) to crash through our thin walls or floor. Afterwards we were quite ready to follow the Semai custom of getting together in a group and maximizing the amount of space and solid material between oneself and a tiger.

Where tigers and elephants are relatively common, the longhouse is the basic living unit. About a quarter of the Semai settlements in the east consist of a single longhouse, a settlement pattern almost never found in the west. A typical west Semai house offers little protection against dangerous animals, which are much rarer in the west. Unless they have the money to buy planks for a Malay-style house, the west Semai usually wall their houses with *atap* and raise them only a couple of feet off the ground.

Raising the house off the ground also has the effect of keeping out some of the more unpleasant ground-dwelling animals. Moreover, a man can install his chicken roosts beneath the floor, so that he can peer through the slats at night to see whether snakes or civet cats are attacking his flock. Nevertheless, Semai houses are considerably less effective against small animals than against large ones. Anyone who opens a storage bag in a Semai house is immediately covered with the cockroaches that have infested it. The Semai are so used to this phenomenon that they do not bother to brush the roaches off. Similarly, at night one always hears the patter and squeaking of house rats. Other animals come into the house to prey on the roaches and rats. There are the house geckoes, small big-eyed lizards called *chi'cha'*, after their rather plaintive call. Yellow and brown spiders with a leg spread about the size of one's palm eat the roaches. Snakes sometimes get into the *atap* roof to search for rats. The Semai custom of dumping garbage through the slatted floors attracts bees and butterflies, which often then fly up into the house. Most of the time one is unaware of the numerous animals in one's house (the list above is not exhaustive), but after a few days' heavy rain, which soaks the *atap* roof, the ceiling begins to crawl with them.

Semai houses are to shelter people against wild animals and the elements, not against the inhabitants' friends and neighbors. The notion of privacy is alien to the east Semai and of little importance to the west Semai. To refuse someone admission to one's house would be an act of extreme hostility and is therefore "taboo" (*punan*). My wife and I had a good deal of trouble getting used to the idea that seeking privacy was aggressive. For example, the east Semai often go to sleep early in the evening. Our house was therefore relatively empty, and we used the evening to type up field notes. The problem was that around five o'clock in the morning some well rested Semai would decide to drop in for a visit. They would cough a few times to see if we were awake or ask in clear, pleasant voices, "You sleeping?" If we pretended to be asleep and they had nothing urgent to do, they would settle down to chat with each other. A person who dropped in by himself might just sit for a while, humming a little tune, or he might rummage through our belongings in hopes of turning up something interesting. At one point we tried tying our door shut. But our east Semai friends would have been shocked and hurt at the idea that there were times when we did not want to see them. Serene in their knowledge that we liked them and were therefore always glad to have them visit, they would reach over the top of the door and untie the fastening. For a while we kept making the binding more and more difficult to untie, but making the binding fantastically complicated delayed their entry by only a few more minutes. Eventually we had to give in to Semai notions of hospitality.

A brief digression on the apparent near absence of a Semai notion of privacy may prove interesting. I think that there are several factors that are conducive to this situation. First, insofar as people do have to band together in time of danger as described above, a strongly developed emphasis on privacy would be an impediment. Second, the construction of traditional Semai houses makes privacy difficult. Because the outside walls are usually thin and the whole house open to the breeze, people near a house can hear what is going on inside. They can also smell what food is being cooked, since the Semai seem to have an acute sense of smell. In the evening after the lights were out we would often chat through the walls for a quarter of an hour or so with any of our next door neighbors who were awake. Similarly, like the changes in the height of the floors, the interior walls in a Semai house serve to mark off areas for certain activities (for example, cooking, sleeping) rather than to shield someone from the curiosity of his housemates. Third, in Semai communities, especially in the east, everyone is at least in part dependent economically on most of the other people in his settlement. He is therefore naturally interested in what they are doing. The population is small enough so that he gets to know them fairly well. Besides, as in most small rural communities, there is very little "news" to talk about, aside from what one's neighbors are up to. Gossip is one of the few entertainments available. Finally, the lack of privacy serves an important social function. There are very few ways in which a Semai can be forced to conform to the standards of his community (see Chapter 7 for more details on this subject). But each person knows that his neighbors are watching him. If he does such a simple thing as start for the river to defecate or bathe, someone is going to ask him where he is going and what he intends to do there. It is quite possible that, after hearing the answer, the questioner will decide to come along too. If a man does something that offends one of his neighbors, the news will be all over the settlement by bedtime. For example, "Goiter says Flower took more than her fair share of the fish the women caught. Besides, said Goiter, Flower has bulgy eyes and a flat nose." In an

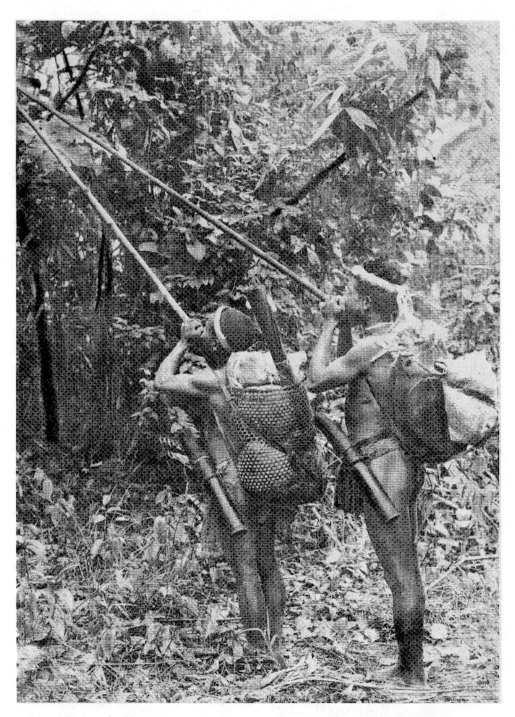

Using the blowpipe (1930s). (Photograph courtesy of Louis Carrard)

hour or two, this news reaches Flower. Goiter then hears, "Flower says anything Goiter says about her will bounce back on Goiter. If Goiter says Flower has bulgy eyes, Goiter has bulgy eyes. If Goiter says Flower has a flat nose, Goiter has a flat nose." Rather than risk being caught up in an exchange of malicious gossip like this, people tend to be rather careful about conforming to their neighbors' notions of proper behavior. Privacy would render gossip less effective as a means of social control.

HUNTING AND TRAPPING   Men hunt with a blowpipe seven or eight feet long. The blowpipe consists of two tubes of bamboo, one inside the other so that the weapon will not bend of its own weight. Semai men treat their blowpipes as symbols of virility. They spend more time making a blowpipe than building a house. After it is made, they lavish yet more time polishing and ornamenting it. Young west Semai boys in villages where no one uses a blowpipe any longer will spend hours playing with a blowpipe brought in by a visitor.

The blowpipe shoots small, featherless darts, the tips of which are smeared with a sticky poison compounded from the *Strychnos* vine, the sap of the upas tree, and such other poisons as toadskin and snake venom. Dart poison, say the Semai, can be made of anything the eating of which makes one sick. Although this principle, derived from years of observation and experiment, is "unscientific," it works pretty well for the Semai, in part because they usually use a mixture of poisons. The dart is notched twice near the end so that if the animal succeeds in brushing the dart off, the point will break and stay imbedded in the wound. The poison does not affect the edibility of the meat except in a small area around the wound and is ineffective against animals much larger than a middle-sized pig.

No weapon can compete with the blowpipe on an emotional level. On the economic level, however, the blowpipe is less important than the shotgun. Long available in the west, shotguns first became widely available in the east during the abortive Communist rebellion in the 1950s when the government distributed them for use against the rebels. The Semai, as unwarlike a people as one could imagine, preferred to use them for hunting. Since the Semai are ignorant of game laws and impossible to supervise anyway, the Game Department is constantly embroiled with Semai "poachers." The government remains unwilling to withdraw the guns, however, for fear of losing the loyalty of the Semai.

Because of the difficulty of travel in the rain forest, a hunter has to be in top physical shape and usually is between twenty-five and forty years old. Older men tend to retire as it were, and become fishermen.

A hunting party usually consists of one to three men, often housemates or brothers, who decide early in the morning to go out hunting. They start out around 7:30 A.M. and try to get back before noon, that is, before the day gets too hot. During fruit season, the hunters may wait underneath a fruit tree for the prey to come to them. More typically, however, the party roves along the paths, occasionally beating the bush a little, until they hear some animal moving. The less experienced hunter then freezes, while his partner goes off to try to get to the other side of the animal. He moves in a crouch with knees slightly bent, very slowly, to avoid frightening the prey further. When he sees the animal, he inserts a dart in the lower end of his blowpipe, stuffs in a little tree cotton so that the dart will not fall out, stands on his toes and raises the blowpipe to his lips. Then he fires. If the animal flees past the waiting hunter, he fires, too. Both then trail the animal by ear until the poison takes effect or the hunters get another clear shot. The hunt generates so much excitement that, when concealment is unnecessary—as, for example, when the prey has taken refuge in the top of a forest giant above the main canopy of the rain forest, thus depriving itself of further refuge—the normally reserved Semai dance around whooping and laughing like children.

There are several minor kinds of hunting. In one, the hunter fans smoke into a hole until the animal comes out or suffocates. In another, a noose on the end of a pole is used to catch arboreal animals like monitor lizards. Occasionally, people go hunting pigs with spears, but the spear is primarily a defensive weapon kept in the house for potential use against wild animals, supernatural beings and what the west Semai call *gengster* (that is, gangsters).

Trapping provides more food than hunting does. The Semai make at least sixteen different kinds of traps, of which only the two most important types are discussed here.

The spring-spear consists of a thick sapling up to 20 feet long pegged back into the shape of a "U." One end is embedded in the ground and the other end is secured by a palm fiber trip string. A razor-sharp bamboo spear is tied on at a right angle to the free arm of the "U," with the tip pointing away from the "U." When an animal stumbles against the trip string, the bent sapling straightens out, snapping the spear into the prey. The Semai mark each trap by trimming a sapling and bending it towards the trap. The spring spear can kill large animals and, during the unsuccessful Communist insurrection, severely wounded both guerrilla and government troops. Although the trap is now outlawed, some east Semai continue to set it along rain forest paths, primarily to catch pigs and deer. The spring-spear more often maims than kills, and in the two to four days between inspections the prey may escape, either to become dangerous or to die unretrieved in some out-of-the-way place.

More efficient and productive are the various noose traps. The noose is either laid flat on the ground or, oftener, suspended from a rattan frame. Whenever possible, the noose is made of wire, but this material is scarce in the east, and people usually have to settle for rattan or palm-fiber string. A man will set a string of five to ten noose traps along animal runs, near burrows or drinking places, preferably either near his house or along the path he takes to his field. Noose traps are also set in fruiting trees.

FISHING   The commonest methods of fishing, more or less in order of popularity, are as follows: trapping, basket fishing, line fishing, poisoning, spearing, netting, and catching by hand. The order varies from place to place, because there is considerable difference between techniques adapted to the small, swift highland brooks and those suited to the large, relatively sluggish lowland rivers.

Fish traps and weirs provide the bulk of the fish, especially in the lowlands. There are almost as many different types of fish traps as of land traps. The commonest type is ovate with a narrow spiked funnel of a mouth through which the fish enters and cannot return. A typical east Semai family has one to three basket traps, but along the Perak River in the west the number may run as high as forty. The smaller traps are set in small streams early in the afternoon and the catch collected next morning. Traps 6 to 10 feet long are set in rivers and inspected every couple of days or so.

A group of three to five men, usually housemates or kinsmen, will build a wall around an abatis of brush felled while clearing a field. They set basket traps at the entrance of the pen thus formed, then throw the trash ashore, scaring the fish into the traps. Similarly, they may pen a deep hole in a stream and then jump into the hole, again scaring the fish into the trap. Along the banks of major rivers, groups of up to a dozen men may construct "fish farms"—pens open at both ends, with fish traps at one end and a door at the other. When the pen is full, the door is closed and people frighten the fish into the traps. "Fish farms" are usually built when the fish are migrating downstream at the beginning of the dry season or upstream at the beginning of the wet season. After a heavy rain, a couple of men may erect a temporary weir across the delta of a tributary stream to trap deep-water fish that have gone into the temporarily deep waters of the tributary. A large party goes out with torches that night to spear the trapped fish Finally, a man and his wife will dam a small stream with rocks, leaving an opening in which a fish trap is set. They then beat a restricted area of the stream above the dam, take their catch and move upstream to repeat the process. Such an expedition will take all morning.

It is usually the women who catch fish in baskets. The fisherwomen put the basket downstream from a pile of half-submerged jetsam and then scatter the pile downstream, catching in their basket the debris and fish hiding there. Basket fishing parties start out early in the morning and return late in the afternoon. The fish caught this way are small, including many of the species sold in American tropical-fish stores. After the catch has been divided equally among the members of a fishing party, there is rarely more than a couple of fish per person.

Line fishing is primarily a man's job and has some of the recreational quality of hunting. Fish poisoning is rather uncommon. Fishing with Malay chain-weighted circular throwing nets is becoming commoner, but most of the east Semai cannot afford to acquire such nets. Fishing by hand, sometimes combined with the use of mild fish poisons, is mostly a children's game. In the west, along the Perak River, most children over six are expert at catching fish by hand. Adult Semai sometimes catch fish for lunch by hand while defecating in small streams.

Keeping Animals

Traditionally, no Semai would kill an animal he had raised but would exchange it with a person in another village, knowing that that person would kill the animal. Even now the Semai rarely kill their animals but raise them for barter or sale. The buyers are usually Malay or Chinese traders.

The commonest domesticated animal is the chicken. Although the Semai have long had chickens, they still domesticate the chicks of the wild jungle fowl, either by clipping their tailfeathers and letting them run with the other chicks as semi-pets or by hatching out wild fowl eggs under their own chickens. Young chicks are kept indoors under an inverted backbasket until able to fend for themselves. Most chickens become prey to disease, snakes, or civet cats before reaching maturity. Because the population is inbred, there are a great many odd-looking chickens with crests instead of combs, bald heads and necks and/or dwarfish legs.

The next commonest domesticated animal is the dog. The aboriginal Semai dog is a small, inbred, orange animal which closely resembles the dogs found in Southeast Asian neolithic sites. This dimunitive animal is too small to be much help in hunting except to call attention to the presence of an animal by barking. (Actually the bark is more like a roar.) In the west this breed has been almost completely replaced by the larger Southeast Asian mongrels known as "pye dogs." Dogs are named and sometimes addressed as "child."

Cats, ducks, and goats are relatively recent introductions. Those west Semai who raise irrigated rice also have water buffalo.

Besides young domesitcated animals, which they treat as pets, the Semai make pets of immature wild animals. Animals treated as pets include mice, monkeys, tigers, squirrels, pigs, otters, civet cats, rats, flying foxes, tortoises and, according to one man, monitor lizards. Birds kept as pets include doves, pigeons, game birds, and kingfishers. The Semai talk and whistle to tame birds and they fondle chicks. They behave yet more affectionately to four-footed pets. They adopt young animals as eagerly as they adopt children, fondle them as they fondle children, address them as "children," give them names, and even suckle them. They seem to lose their interest in pets as the animals mature, and most adult pets escape into the rain forest. Adult monkeys, however, are sometimes kept chained in or under the house. Pets are rarely sold and never eaten.

Semai Zoology

TAXONOMY Understanding the system of taboos called *pǝnali'* is impossible without understanding the logical basis of the way in which the Semai classify and conceptualize the organisms involved. Different conceptual systems "pay attention" to different attributes of their universe. For example, Euro-Americans classify whales as mammals, paying attention to such attributes as warm blood and suckling the young, but at one time many people classified whales as fish, paying attention to characteristics such as shape and habitat. Although the number of characteristics to which a conceptual system can pay attention is finite, it is large enough to allow many different ways of classifying the same set of facts. The first step in understanding this Semai conceptual system is, therefore, to try to determine the characteristics on which its classification rests.

For the Semai, a "real meal" consists of meat, fish, fowl, or fungus, plus a starchy food like rice or tapioca. A man who has not had meat, fish, fowl, or fungus recently will say, with complete seriousness, "I haven't eaten for days." The words "meat," "fish," "fowl," and "fungus," however, are imprecise translations of the Semai words. My impression is that the Semai classification involves three main principles.

First, the Semai categories seem to be based on where the organism lives rather than on what it looks like. *Cheb* are air animals (that is, birds), and *ka'* are water animals (fish, and, in the east, turtles and water snails). Land organisms in this "real food" system are *bǝtiis* (fleshy fungi) or *mǝnhar* (meat). The Semai describe the taste of fungi as like meat, fowl, or fish rather than like other vegetables. It is therefore logical to put them in the meat-fowl-fish system. On the other hand, fungi are obviously different from animals (for example, they don't move around the way animals do). In fact, they seem to be too different to lump together with land animals as *mɘnhar*. The Semai distinguish three types of land animals, again on the basis of habitat: "those beneath the earth" (snakes and lizards), tree *mɘnhar* (such as squirrels and monkeys) and land *mɘnhar* (for example, deer and pig).

Animals that live in two habitats are arbitrarily assigned to one or the other. Thus bats are "tree *mɘnhar*," and for the east Semai frogs and toads are *ka'*. Land tortoises are also *ka'* for the east Semai, probably because they look like water turtles.

The problem with doing an analysis of this sort is that, like most peoples, the Semai find their own conceptual scheme so obvious that they have trouble explaining the defining characteristics of these categories to a non-Semai. Knowing that his informants may not be able to help him out, an anthropologist guides his analysis of conceptual schemes by the rule that the simplest explanation of the most facts is the best explanation. Now, the analysis just given is "two-dimensional." One dimension is habitat, and the other, the one that distinguishes fungi from meat, seems to be something like mobility. But suppose that the real basis of the system is locomotion, that is, *cheb* fly, *ka'* swim, *bɘtiis* do not move, and *mɘnhar* walk. Similarly, snakes and lizards wriggle, ground *mɘnhar* walk, and tree *mɘnhar* climb. This one-dimensional explanation is simpler, more "parsimonious," as logicians say. Yet I am inclined to favor the more complicated one, because I think it ties in more closely with the way the Semai talk about the organisms in the various categories. Which analysis is right is a question that must go unanswered until someone can talk with an exceptionally intellectual and perceptive Semai.

The second principle in the way the Semai think about animals is still harder to discover. My impression is that the Semai think that some species are more "typical" of their categories than other species are. For example, *naga'* (snakelike dragons) seem to represent the quintessence of "they beneath the earth." Giant monitors, in turn, are the prime representative of "lizard," and regal python of "snake." There is also some evidence that the Semai have a feeling that animals in different habitats should have different sorts of skin: *cheb*, feathers; *ka'* rounded scales or moist skins; tree *mɘnhar*, fur like human head hair; land *mɘnhar*, hair like human body hair; and "they beneath the earth," scales that form a pattern of diamonds "like a backbasket." Animals which do not meet these expectations are apparently felt to be anomalous, odd, "unnatural."

Obviously, one has to be wary in dealing with things that do not fit neatly into the natural order. People say, for example, that one should be very careful about eating anomalous animals, especially in situations that are already dangerous enough (such as, during pregnancy). For example, the "flying lemur" is "tree *mɘnhar*," closely related to monkeys; but it "flies" like a *cheb*. Similarly, the pangolin is *mɘnhar*. but covered with large overlapping scales like a *ka'*. The meat of these two animals should not be mixed with *any* other meat, and there are several other rules about cooking and eating it. Snakes are another instance of animals that do not fit neatly into Semai taxonomy. *Mɘnhar* should be quadrupedal. The Semai say that a snake has "a bad body." Asked what he meant by "a bad body," one Semai man explained, "It has no arms, it has no legs and it scares me." Among the east Semai there are many restrictions (la'na') on eating snakes, and the west Semai do not eat snakes at all. The rules and restrictions about eating such anomalous foods seem to be ways of handling the dangers inherent in eating "unnatural" things. This response holds not only for the broad categories already described but also for smaller subcategories. For example, the Semai idea of what a "snake" should look like resembles that of most Euro-Americans. The short python (*Python curtus*) has a very short tail and looks much stubbier than most other snakes. The east Semai, who cannot afford to pass up the meat of such a large animal (up to 9 feet long), observe many restrictions on eating short python and insist, wrongly, that the animal is very venomous. Similarly, the eyelessness of the blind snakes mentioned in Chapter 2 seems to violate the Semai notion of what snakes should look like. I once picked up one of these little snakes in the river and brought it home for identification. People jammed the doorway of our house to see the "headband of Thunder" (also called "spawn of the sun"). No one would come within a yard or two of the specimen, however, for fear of bringing on a disaster (tɔrlaid). In short, if an animal does not look the way the Semai say that animals in that category should look, then it makes the Semai uneasy and they treat it with great care.

The final principle in this system is that some foods are more dangerous to eat than others. The more dangerous the food, the more likely it is that people in an already dangerous situation like pregnancy will not eat it. Within any category of land animals, the larger an animal is, the more dangerous eating it is. I think that one can also arrange the major food categories in an order of decreasing dangerousness, although there are a good many exceptions: land mɔnhar, tree mɔnhar, birds, ka', and fungi. I feel that this hypothetical sequence may mirror an unconscious sense on the part of the Semai that, for example, land mɔnhar are much more like human beings than fungi are. If this guess is right, then it would follow that the Semai naturally take more precautions about killing and eating creatures like themselves than about doing the same to relatively inhuman creatures.

Pɔnali'

Like most peoples, the Semai do not regard the way in which they categorize the world as arbitrary. The four major categories of "real food" and the three subdivisions of mɔnhar are taken to be part of the natural order. Logically, then, mixing together foods from different categories is mixing up the natural order, an impious violation of the nature of the world. Therefore eating or cooking foods from different categories is going to bring on some further reverberation in the natural order. Just how serious the disturbance in the natural order will be depends on how dangerous the animal is to eat. Mixing pork with other foods might bring on an epidemic of infectious hepatitis or a violent thundersquall, while mixing fungi and fish would probably lead only to baldness or pains in one's back. In order to avoid upsetting the natural order this way, the Semai observe a "taboo" (pɔnali') on eating or cooking foods from different categories at the same time. Eating steak smothered in mushrooms, for example, would be pɔnali'. People would say that a

Semai who ate such a dish was "eating *rawoid.*" The word *rawoid* seems to be cognate with the word *roid,* "to lose one's bearings, to get lost and wander around." Incoherent babbling that follows none of the rules of proper discourse is "talking *rawoid.*" Eating *rawoid* thus seems to mean something like "eating without regard to the orderly processes of nature."

Not only should one not actually mix foods from different categories together, one should not even serve them at the same meal. Ideally, a Semai should have a separate set of dishes for each of the four major categories. Although the east Semai, who have few dishes, tend to ignore this refinement, most west Semai have at least two sets of dishes. If a person does not have enough dishes, serving *mənhar* on a banana-leaf plate is far safer than serving it in a dish that once held *Ka',* no matter how well the dish has been scrubbed. Furthermore, after the meal, the dishwater should be dumped in different areas, depending on what sort of food has been served.

The west Semai know that Chinese and Englishmen eat "mixed" (*pənali'*) foods without any natural disaster following. They explain that non-Semai may "understand" (*tageh*) mixed dishes, having eaten them since childhood. Some young Semai are able to eat Chinese food, they say, because they also have been familiar with it since they were children. It remains dangerous, however, they conclude, since even the English and the Chinese are more likely to get bald than the Semai are, probably because they ignore the rules of *pənali'*.

Nicknames

The east Semai do not use the real "name" of an animal they are hunting or eating. Instead, they use a nickname (*mɔl,* "handle") that belongs to the *ənroo' kərəndei,* "language making-not-to-know." These nicknames have fallen into disuse in the west, with a few exceptions like the nicknames for elephant ("Mr. Big") tiger ("Grandfather Stripes"), crocodile ("Mr. Cigarette"), giant monitor lizard ("Mr. Machete"), and bearcat ("Mr. Fire"). The *ənroo' kərəndei* is a typically Semai way of dealing with dangers posed by the non-Semai world. Instead of defying something that threatens them, the Semai try to deceive it. The basic purpose of the *ənroo' kərəndei* is to keep a Semai-speaking non-Semai from realizing that the Semai are talking about him.

The words in this secret language are formed in one of two ways. First, they may refer to some characteristic of the entity under discussion. For instance, the seductive female "bird spirits" become "They of the Long Hair," a gibbon "Mr. Long Hands," a quail "Rice-Counting Bird," a panggolin "That Thing with Fish Scales" and the circumcized Malays "Clipped People." Some of these nicknames are based on analogies rather obscure to non-Semai. For example, flying lemurs are "Mr. Carry-in-a-Sling" because, in resting position, the animal seems to be supported by its membraneous "wings" in the same way that a Semai child is supported by the sling in which its mother carries it (see photograph). The other way of forming nicknames is to use a word close in sound to the sound of the real "name." For instance, a macaque (*Macaca irus,* called *rau* in Semai and *kera* in Malay) be-

East Semai girl and her baby. The baby's hat cost a large part of the family's income (1962).

comes a *kərenh,* and a Bengali Indian becomes a *Mənggalaint.* Since the Semai delight in word play, this sort of nickname is often a pun. In the presence of a Tamil Indian, for example, the west Semai do not use the normal word for Tamil, *Kəling,* but instead use the word *kəlag,* "bird of prey." Building on this pun, they sometimes use the word "chicken grabbers" (a "handle" for birds of prey) to refer to Tamils.

These nicknames reflect the tendency of the Semai language to use words slightly different in sound to refer to phenomena slightly different in nature, for example, *chəngiis* and *chəngees* refer to two slightly different odors. More important, they exemplify the Semai preference for dealing with non-Semai by obfuscation. Faced with a danger from the non-Semai world, one of the first Semai responses is to work out a way of confusing their potential enemies. For instance, when the west Semai heard that Indonesia had adopted a policy of confrontation with Malaysia and might declare war any day, one of the first actions they took was to think up nicknames for "Indonesian," for example, "Egg People" in reference to the bombs the Indonesians were expected to drop, "Tobacco People" in reference to the fact that one of the better tobaccos smoked in Malaysia comes from Java in Indonesia.

I think that the use of a secret language to refer to animals stems from the fact that the Semai fear the consequences of their own violence (see Chapter 6). In most of their dealings with the animal world they are the aggressors, killing and eating. From the Semai point of view, some sort of violent retaliation is to be expected. They therefore try to conceal what they are doing in a variety of ways. For example, the west Semai will not tease or kill a helpless wounded animal but will let it go free. The secret language seems also to be a way of evading the consequences of aggression by concealing the fact of aggression.

Just what might retaliate against the Semai—that is, just what the secret language is supposed to fool—remains obscure. The nickname should be used from the time hunters are on the trail of an animal until a day or two after the meat has been eaten. Some Semai say that using the real "name" will alert the quarry, but this danger seems slight after the animal has been eaten. Others say that using the "name" while eating the meat would cause cramps, and still others say that the animal's "soul" (*ruai*) or "essence" (*kɔloog*) will respond to its name and wreak vengeance on its slayer. My impression is that the Semai do not make a sharp distinction between a verbal category and an individual in that category. For example, perhaps the reason that people are unsure whether Thunder is singular or plural is that, in a sense, all thunder is immanent in any given case of thunder. In other words, I think that on some unverbalized level the Semai may regard an individual as the embodiment of the linguistic category to which it belongs. The category in turn is not felt to be an arbitrary linguistic phenomenon but at least a faithful reflection and perhaps an actual part of the natural order. To take what may be an analogous example from Euro-American society, a murder is considered not just a crime against the victim but a crime against "mankind," the category to which the victim belongs. "Mankind" in turn is felt to be not just a word but in some sense a real entity. Similarly, I think that, without being able to express their feeling, the Semai may feel that killing a gibbon, say, is not just an act of violence against that gibbon but against "gibbonkind." Insofar as "gibbonkind" is part of the natural order, such an act is dangerous. To deal with this potential danger, people resort to the standard Semai tactic of obfuscation. In short, if this analysis is right, then the vaguely conceptualized thing the Semai try to dupe by using their secret language is the natural order as categorized by the Semai language.

4

Plants and Agriculture

THE SOIL of Semai-land is of low inherent fertility but supports a rich flora of the "Western Malaysian" type. That is, the flora has more in common with that of Sumatra or Borneo than with that of continental Asia. There are far more species of plants in this type of forest than in, say, American woodland. There are, for example, over 8000 species of flowering plants, of which at least 2500 are trees. Stands of a single species are rare. The tree trunks are usually tall (often up to 150 feet) and straight, supported by large buttresses. So great is the competition for living space that trees grow straight out from the banks of rivers parallel to the surface of the water for 10 or 15 feet, and seeds germinate as soon as they hit the ground. As some plants are growing and taking nutrients out of the soil, however, others are dying and returning nutrients to the soil in the form of rotting vegetable matter. The heat and humidity of the Malayan climate speed up this cycle of growth and decay.

When the Semai clear a field, the soil is exposed to the direct rays of the sun. The resulting increase in soil temperature greatly increases the rate at which the humus decomposes. The clearing of the forest cover means that, while Semai crops are taking nutrients out of the soil, no new humus is being laid down. Moreover, the Semai prefer to locate their fields by streams so that traveling to one's field is easy. Because Semai country tends to be hilly, this preference often leads to clearing fields on steep slopes. The result is that the heavy Malayan rains begin to wash away the topsoil, which is no longer protected by a thick forest cover. Consequently, using a field for more than a few years would almost totally destroy the fertility of the soil so that neither crops nor rain forest could grow on it.

The Semai recognize that the second year's crop from a given field is usually less abundant than the first year's. More important, however, is the fact that after a year or two the field is overgrown with weeds and brush. They therefore abandon their fields after a year or so and clear new fields elsewhere. The result is that a new forest cover grows up, the nutrient cycle is re-established, and after about a dozen years the soil has largely regained its fertility.

Agriculture

In deciding where to clear a field, the Semai take the wild plant cover into account. There are four major Semai categories of plant cover. These categories do not correspond exactly to any English categories so that it is necessary to use Semai terms to describe them. An "old field" (*səlai manah*) is a year or two old, still producing some crops. *Pabəl* is thick undergrowth, usually from two to seven years old. *Bəlaki'* is rain forest with a thick layer of undergrowth, typically from seven to twelve years old. Finally, *jərəs* is a rain forest of large trees and little undergrowth, typically over a dozen years old.

For a small field the Semai often clear *pabəl,* because the undergrowth can easily be cut down with a machete. For a large field, people prefer *bəlaki'* to *jərəs.* In *jərəs* the trees are so tall and the buttresses so thick that the men often have to build a scaffold 15 feet high to get to a portion of the trunk thin enough for them to chop through with their small axes (see photograph). Besides, the forest giants do not burn well, with the result that their huge charred trunks sometimes litter the field. Thus, the Semai can plant about 25 to 30 pounds of seed rice in an acre cleared of *bəlaki',* but only about 20 pounds of seed in an acre cleared of *jərəs.* Nevertheless, because the closed cycle that produces humus is restored in *jərəs,* it is more fertile than *bəlaki',* and both are far more fertile than *pabəl,* facts the Semai recognize.

Because crops are so important, the Semai also use magic to help them determine whether or not a given plot of land will be fertile. Semai in different places use different types of magic, but a certain basic procedure underlies the differences. A man clears a very small patch of earth and cleanses it by sprinkling it with a decoction of magic leaves and a magic whisk. He then plants a small stick in the ground. He goes home and if he has a propitious dream, or if the stick has "grown" overnight, he knows that the land will be fertile. I imagine that he has probably unconsciously made up his mind already, and that his dream or the "growing" stick simply serve to make him less anxious about his decision.

The main difference between east and west Semai agriculture is that in the east people resettle every few years near their fields whenever the depletion of the soil has forced them to clear new fields, whereas in the west settlements tend to be more permanent, with people rotating their fields around the village every few years. There seem to be several reasons for this difference. First, some west Semai work for wages and therefore do not clear any fields at all. There is thus more land available near the settlement for people who do want to plant crops. The larger eastern fields use up the arable land around a village more quickly, forcing the people to clear new land elsewhere. Second, in some low-lying western areas the Semai grow irrigated rice, which gives a much higher yield per acre than the hill rice grown by most other Semai. They can therefore get the same amount of rice from smaller fields. Conversely, some of the highland Semai in the east still depend on foxtail millet, which has a much lower yield per acre than even hill rice, with the result that settlements there have to move almost every year. Third, west Semai sometimes plant rubber trees and orchards of fruit trees, which take several years to mature.

East Semai man felling a tree (1962).

Moreover, with the money they can earn they buy bulky things like clocks with visible pendulums (a favorite item) or planks to build permanent Malay-style houses. Owning trees and bulky durable goods and/or having jobs means that resettling would be a difficult task, necessitating serious economic losses. The east Semai do not plant trees, have few bulky material possessions, and erect houses so flimsy that they must be rebuilt every two or three years, whether or not the settlement is moved. They are thus much freer to move than the westerners. Fourth, while the east Semai are fairly isolated, many of the west Semai live near Chinese and Malays. The Chinese and Malays also grow crops, with the result that there is often no unused arable land for the Semai to move to. In the east, there is far more unused land than the Semai need. Fifth, the west Semai are gradually becoming dependent on the luxuries of Chinese-Malay society, like hospitals, movies, and schools. One west Semai settlement has remained near a Chinese town for over a decade simply so that they and adjacent Semai settlements will have a convenient home base from which to send children to a local school. The east Semai still have little access to such amenities. Sixth, while the east Semai are so afraid of strangers that they sometimes flee from the sound of a motorboat coming upstream into their territory, the west Semai have become used to living near Chinese and Malays. The westerners still suspect that non-Semai have evil intentions, but they will not resettle simply to get away from them. Finally, the east Semai will abandon a settlement in which two or three people have died (see Chapter 9). The west Semai have given up this custom. In short, for a variety of reasons the west Semai site their fields near their settlements, while the east Semai site their settlements near their fields.

There is no permanent ownership of fields among the Semai. A nuclear family "owns" land which they have cleared and from which they are still getting crops. The fields are usually marked off into nuclear family plots by fallen logs or lines-of-sight between two landmarks. If for some reason a man is unable to clear a plot, he asks for part of the field of a kinsman or housemate. As will be seen later, to refuse such a request would be *punan,* an extremely serious breach of proper behavior. If someone outside the nuclear family helps clear a family plot, the head of the family supplies him with tobacco and feeds him a meal when the work is finished or gives him some rice and tobacco to take home. Young men with no children usually help to work the fields of the nuclear family with whom they eat. Before a settlement moves, people clear fields near the site of the new settlement, which may be a couple of miles from the old one.

The east Semai clear their fields twice a year, the west Semai only once. The easterners clear "little fields" shortly after the harvest from the "big fields" is in, usually in January. Most of the time only a minority of families in an eastern settlement clear "little fields."

Because of climatic variation, the calendar dates for clearing "big fields" vary from place to place. The important thing is that it should be done by the end of the dry season so that the fallen bushes and trees will be dry enough to burn, but the new crops will then get the benefit of the monsoon rains. The Semai figure that it is time to begin clearing fields when a certain kind of tree called *pərah* (*Elateriospermum tapos*) puts out new leaves. Clearing starts in April, May, or June and is finished two to three months later.

Women and children usually start the process of clearing, by slashing the undergrowth with machetes. After the first two days, the workers are supposed to take a day off. In *jarɔs,* where there is little undergrowth, it takes about two weeks to clear a "big field" of bush; in *bɔlaki',* where undergrowth is thicker, it takes about a month. In *pabɔl,* where there is nothing but undergrowth, a vigorous man can clear an acre in a week or so. Clearing the undergrowth usually results in the discovery of bush-dwelling rodents or bats, which go into the cooking pot. The heaps of fallen brushwood in the streams near the field serve as shelters for fish and are exploited in basket fishing (see Chapter 3).

When the undergrowth is cleared, the men fell the large trees with axes. Usually the trees at the top of the hill are felled first so that large trees will, in falling, carry down the smaller ones below them, which are often notched first. To fell five or six trees at once this way requires an expert and is considered great fun. Since felling a forest giant takes two men at least a whole morning, its fall is usually the sign to quit for the day, or, in the case of exceptionally energetic axe-men, to take a break for lunch and a cooling dip in a nearby stream. Felling an acre of *jarɔs* takes two to four weeks.

Depending on the rainfall, the felled brush and trees must be left to dry for a month or six weeks before it is burnable. Ideally, there should be a week without rain before the burning. Because of the constant danger that more rain will fall on nearly dry fields, however, people become anxious. Therefore, even if the fields are not thoroughly dry, when one man burns his field his covillagers usually follow suit. The sight of the smoke from burning fields is likely to start a chain reaction in settlements up and down the river.

As a result, the initial burning is often incomplete, leaving as much as a third of the field to be re-burnt. Before the second burning, people pile the smaller logs and scraps over and parallel to the larger unburnt logs. When the piles burn, they leave a rich deposit of ash on which certain minor crops—for example, hot peppers, chives, lemongrass, and tobacco—are planted. After the final burning, there is a mandatory cooling period, two to four days if it rains heavily, up to a week or more otherwise. If planting began while the fields were still hot, the heat of the soil would kill the plants as it does the weeds.

The organization of labor in planting crops is much like that for clearing, except that the work groups tend to be larger and the expense of paying them off with rice and tobacco that much greater. There is a preplanting ritual much like the preclearing ritual, and the planters put in fragrant magical plants "to help the rice grow." The only tool used in planting is a pointed staff which anthropologists call a "dibble" or "dibbling stick." The men and boys usually do the actual dibbling, making holes with the dibble into which the women and girls drop half-a-dozen rice seeds or a stem-cutting of tapioca or a half-grown tobacco plant, and so on. In the case of minor crops, however, a man or woman may do both the dibbling and the planting.

Since a Semai usually does not devote any part of his field exclusively to a single crop, several different kinds of crops are planted in each section of the field. During the early days of the Communist uprising in Malaya, before the rebels realized what was happening and began to follow the Semai pattern, Semai intercropping allowed the pilots of British reconnaissance planes to distinguish Semai fields from the neatly arranged fields of the guerrillas. In some cases, however, the Semai tend to plant rice or maize in the center of their fields, with tapioca around the edges.

Rice is usually planted first. The planter holds the seeds in his or her left fist and lets just the right number drop into the right palm, which flicks them into the hole made by the dibble. The next crop to be planted is maize. Tapioca and the other crops are last. No fertilizers are used. The Semai describe the use of fecal material on fields as revolting. In fact, common slang terms for Chinese are "Excrement People" and "Urine People," because the Chinese do use excrement to fertilize their fields.

Since most of the fields of the east Semai are cleared in *bɔlaki'* or *jɔrɔs*, there is usually enough fuel to generate enough heat to sterilize the topsoil and thus inhabit weed growth. Besides, the Semai think weeding is grubby and boring. The east Semai therefore do little to prevent weeds from growing among their crops. Since the maturing crops attract animals from the surrounding rain forest, the fields are at this time a favored location for traps and for grasshopper hunts. The Semai, however, regard these traps and hunts as ways of getting food rather than as ways to protect crops. Even when a man stands guard with a shotgun at night to kill raiding deer or wild pigs, thoughts of meat are uppermost in his mind. The Semai say that sometimes they build huge deadfalls to kill marauding elephants, but the only response we saw was their retirement to the sturdiest houses in the settlement until the elephants moved on.

Among the west Semai, land pressure from surrounding Malays and Chinese often forces people to clear fields in *pabɔl*. As a result, there is often not enough fuel to kill the weeds when the fields are burnt. The Semai say that weeding is the hardest agricultural task. Given the extraordinary reproductive powers of Malayan plants, a man and his wife can keep no more than an acre fairly free of weeds. In larger fields, weeds tend to grow faster than they can be pulled up. The result is that a nuclear family clears only an acre or two. Moreover, field pests firmly established in the permanent Malay and Chinese fields come to attack west Semai crops in greater numbers than they do in the east. To protect their crops without moving their villages, the west Semai erect temporary houses in the fields, from which they operate bird-scaring devices. A couple of women or children may sleep two or three nights in a row in the field house around harvest time, when the crops are especially attractive to field pests. Rather than sleep alone, however, an individual will make a daily trek to his or her field, returning at night to the permanent settlement to sleep. Since the west Semai buy a good deal of food and have adopted some of the Malay attitudes toward food animals, they tend not to eat field pests. When the rice is "pregnant," that is, beginning to bear, the west Semai traditionally sprinkle it with the acidic juice squeezed from the fruit of a stemless palm (*Zalacca conferta*) because, they say, "pregnant people like acidic foods."

The first crop to become ripe is amaranth, whose leaves the Semai boil to make a kind of spinach eaten with rice or tapioca. Next come maize, squash, and rice, in that order. The rice harvest is by far the most organized part of the harvest. After performing a brief ritual, the women harvest the rice with machetes or with special Malay-style "rice knives," which can be hidden in the hand. Use of the lat-

West Semai woman preparing to pound rice. The mat is to catch any grains that fall from the mortar (1963).

ter, according to a Malay belief to which some Semai subscribe, keeps the "soul of the rice" from being frightened. A hard worker can harvest 18 to 20 pounds of hill rice an hour. Wet-rice harvesters can get three or four times as much in the same amount of time from their more densely crowded crop. The severed rice ears are dried on mats in the village or by the field house.

The harvested ears of grain are put on mats near the field or in the settlement. Young men and occasionally women tread the ears, repeatedly turning them over with their bare feet. The resulting friction frees the grain from the ear. The women pound the freed grain in wooden mortars to remove the husk from the grain. They then winnow away the chaff by tossing the mixture of broken husks and grain up and down in a winnowing basket.

After the rice harvest, each west Semai nuclear family throws a party for a score of relatives and neighbors. All Semai settlements, both east and west, have a village-wide harvest feast from which strangers are in theory excluded, although no one would refuse to give a visitor food. At these feasts people get almost ten pounds of rice apiece in the course of visiting from house to house. The west Semai have also taken over a rice harvest ceremony from the Malays.

A Conjectural History of Semai Agriculture

In the distant past the Semai probably exploited the rain forest the way the Semang still do, by collecting wild vegetables, roots, and fruits. Even now, if a woman notices a patch of edible mushrooms or ferns, she will collect them, wrap them in a moist leaf to keep them fresh, and take them home to stew for the next meal. Present-day Semai rarely dig up wild roots except in emergencies. Should the crops fail, however, they know where to find patches of yams, especially the giant *takuub* yam (*Dioscorea orbiculata, D. pyrifolia*) whose tuber is often over 6 feet long. It may take all day for a group of men using machetes and dibbles to dig up a single *takuub* tuber and carry it home. Fruits are today the most important wild plant food that the Semai gather. The favorite fruits are the oily *parah* (*Elateriospermum tapos*), the foul-smelling but delicious durian, and the wild breadfruit. In collecting fruits the Semai use either their hands or a fruit crook, which knocks the fruit loose or pulls down the branches to within plucking distance. If the fruit is highly prized and the tree too hard to climb (for example, durian), people will clear a small area under the tree during fruit season and settle down in a temporary lean-to. When the ripe fruit falls, the waiting Semai rush out to collect it before rats, squirrels, or tigers eat it.

It is easy to see how agriculture could grow out of these activities. Like the Semang, the Semai tend wild yam patches. Furthermore, they eat fruits seed and all, so that automatically fertilized undigested seeds sprout up in the area around a Semai settlement. Naturally, on returning to the area, people tend to settle near these "encouraged" plants. Presumably they followed these patterns in their preagricultural past.

The next step may have been actually to plant seeds and tubers before roving off in the constant search for food, a step taken in the last few decades by several groups of Semang. The first crops were probably the indigenous yams, taro (another large tuber), and bananas. The first cereal crop seems to have been Job's tears, which the east Semai call the "mother of foxtail millet." Next came the foxtail millet itself. Some time after the Portuguese first contacted Malaya in the fifteenth century A.D., the Semai acquired four American crops: maize, tapioca, sweet potatoes, and tobacco. Maize has a much higher yield than foxtail millet and, unlike millet, can be harvested twice a year. Although the Semai find tapioca unappetizing and bland, this root crop has two advantages over yams and taro. First, tapioca roots do not rot if left in the ground so that there is no need to rush to get the harvest in at any specific time. Second, tapioca produces more food per acre than any other crop. The result, in the Semai case, was that maize and tapioca became staple foods, replacing millet and yams. No one is sure when rice first reached the west Semai, but the east Semai began planting it only about fifty years ago. It is now the major food in most of Semai country, with tapioca taking its place when the rice harvest is exhausted. Nevertheless, the Semai persist in growing their old crops and in growing as many varieties of each crop as they have available. The reason, they explain, is that if any set of crops fails, there will always be at least some type of crop that survives.

5

Economics and Daily Life

The Use of Food

DISTRIBUTION OF FOOD   People familiar only with industrial economies often find it hard to understand systems of distribution in nonindustrial economies like that of the Semai. Since, especially in the east where formal political structures are almost completely lacking, the system by which the Semai distribute food and services is one of the most significant ways in which members of a community are knit together, an understanding of this aspect of Semai economy is crucial to a comprehension of how Semai society holds together. A contrast between industrial and Semai systems of distribution may help clarify the dynamics of the latter.

In an industrial society A gives B money and B in turn gives A goods or services. As in a two-handed poker game, A's gain is B's loss and vice versa. Ideally, all gains and losses should add up to zero. If A's gain and B's gain are not the same, then either A or B has "cheated." To guard against cheating, both parties calculate gains and losses very closely, using money as their measuring device.

In many industrial societies, however, another sort of economic exchange takes place, although people tend not to recognize it as economic. For example, people exchange "gifts" at Christmas. Here one is supposed *not* to calculate gains and losses. Although some people do calculate, ideally "it's the thought that counts." Christmas exchanges are just as "economic" as commercial exchanges; and Semai economic exchanges are more like Christmas exchanges than like commercial exchanges.

Take a specific example. After several days of fruitless hunting, an east Semai man kills a large pig. He lugs it back through the moist heat to his settlement. Everyone gathers around. Two other men meticulously divide the pig into portions sufficient to feed two adults each. (Children are not supposed to eat pork.) As nearly as possible each portion contains exactly the same amount of meat, fat, liver, and innards as every other portion. It takes a couple of hours to cut the pig up into portions that are exactly equal. The adult men of the house groups take the leaf-wrapped portions home to redistribute them among the members of the house group (for the composition of the house group, see Chapter 4).

The question that immediately occurs to people brought up in a commercial society is, "What does the hunter get out of it?" The answer is that he and his wife get a portion exactly the same size as anyone else gets. No one even says "thanks." In fact, as will become clear, saying "thanks" would be very rude. Moreover, whereas in some societies the hunter would gain prestige, in east Semai society he is treated like everyone else. In fact, he is probably too young to get the deference due his elders.

The rules governing this type of distribution are obviously not commercial. The first rule is that calculating the amount of a gift is "taboo" (*punan*). The second rule is to share whatever one can afford. If one has only a little surplus over one's own immediate needs, one shares with one's nuclear family; if more, with people in one's house or neighboring houses; if a large amount, with all the people in one's settlement. One must also share with guests and with anyone who asks. Not to share is *punan*. The final rule is that it is *punan* either to refuse a request or to ask for more than the donor can afford. Because of this last rule, people rarely ask outright for gifts for fear of putting the donor in *punan*. A person may drop in at mealtime, however, in hopes of getting some food. If no one offers him any, he may remark casually, often averting his eyes, "I haven't had a good meal in days." If the diners have enough, they invite him to eat. Otherwise, since he has not specifically asked, they may ignore him without running the danger of *punan*.

There are, of course, "stingy" and "selfish" people who do not share what they can afford. Few Semai will call themselves "stingy" or "selfish," however, and sometimes people will continue to share food with a "stingy" person for fear of seeming to calculate gains and losses. On the other hand, although "generosity" is the mark of a "good heart," sharing more than one can afford is plain "dumb." In this context saying thank you is very rude, for it suggests, first, that one has calculated the amount of a gift and, second, that one did not expect the donor to be so generous. In fact, saying thank you is *punan*.

The intriguing aspect of this system is that direct exchanges of goods between A and B are *punan*. At any given time A gives to B, C, D, and so on. As in a Monopoly game, everyone but A profits. However, B, C, and D also have to share with A when they get a surplus. For example, A shares a pig with B, C, D, and others; B shares a python with A, C, D, and others; C shares a deer with A, B, D, and others. Some people give less to A than A gives them; others give more. In the long run, A gets back from the *group* of people with whom he shares roughly the equivalent of what he has given them, though in his exchanges with any specific person he may lose more than he gains or vice versa. In short, the economic system ties a Semai to a whole group of people, and, conversely, groups of Semai are bound together by economic ties.

Furthermore, if A gets back from the other people roughly what he has shared with them, he actually profits. If he kept his pig to himself, for example, the meat would go bad long before he could eat it all. When he gives it away, it is all eaten; he then receives an equivalent amount of meat back over a long period of time so that he can eat it without spoilage. Instead of a man's getting too much food at a single time, followed by a long period of scarcity, this sharing system spaces out small portions of food over the same length of time. Since a person receives in small portions about the same amount of food he contributes in large amounts, he actually is able to consume more meat than he could have done if he did not share. The total amount of food available to the group within which food is shared is greater than the amount that would be available to all the individual members had they tried to consume it individually. Everyone profits by this system.

The result is that an east Semai individual will contribute his food to the general store not merely because he thinks it right to do so but also because it is to his advantage. The sharing of food involves economic ties that make Semai groups more stable than they might otherwise be. Furthermore, a man can rely on his associates' sharing food with him because their sharing ultimately benefits themselves.

The introduction of money has a devastating effect on this aboriginal Semai economy. As a universal standard of value, money necessarily introduces the forbidden element of calculation into economic exchanges. Moreover, money, unlike food, does not spoil so that sharing does not increase the amount of wealth available. Finally, it is much easier to hide money than food so that identifying "selfish" people becomes harder. Consequently the east Semai are beginning to exempt money (and, in some cases, things bought with money) from the rules governing the distribution of food.

The west Semai, most of whom use money and often buy food in a Malay-Chinese market, still share food with close kinsmen or within the household and the neighboring households of kinsmen. Outside these relatively narrow circles, however, people may actually sell food to each other, for example, to a nonkinsman who lives on the other side of the settlement. Moreover, since buying food permits close calculation of how much one needs, there is often no surplus over the immediate needs of a given nuclear family or household so that there is in fact nothing to share. A man who is generous to people who are not close kinsmen and/or nearby neighbors can thus gain prestige among the west Semai. Instead of receiving food for food, in other words, he receives a good reputation. In short, although the economy tends to bind together fairly large groups of east Semai, its effects are limited to smaller groups of west Semai.

PREPARING AND EATING FOOD   Both men and women cook, thresh and winnow grain, grate tapioca roots to make "bread," and so forth. Ordinarily, however, the women do much more of this work than the men. For example, men usually cook only on special occasions or when they are hungry and there is no woman around who will cook for them.

For the Semai the point of eating is to feel "full" (*bɔhei'*). For a meal to be filling it must include a starch dish, preferably rice. When rice is scarce, roasted or boiled tapioca root may be substituted, but people say that tapioca is less filling and therefore does not make as good a meal. To eat meat, fowl, or fish without a starch dish is ridiculous in Semai opinion. "What do you think we are, cats?"

The traditional way of preparing meat, fish, or fowl is to fill a green bamboo tube with alternate layers of flesh and tapioca, adding water and the appropriate spices. The cook then stuffs leaves into the mouth of the tube so that it will not spill and puts the tube into the fire, rotating it occasionally until it is charred black all over. Small pieces of flesh may be stewed with leafy vegetables or wrapped in a leaf and roasted in the embers. When other side dishes for the starch are unavailable a Semai may have to be content with grinding chili peppers and salt together to add piquancy to the meal. Now people usually cook rice in Malay-style cooking pots.

Traditionally, men, women, and children ate together with little or no formality. Now, however, people are beginning to adopt such Malay refinements as washing their hands before the meal, using only their right hand to eat and so forth. Although there are no set meal times, the west Semai are beginning to follow the Malay pattern of three meals a day.

Daily Cycle

The idea of meticulous punctuality is far less important in Semai life than it is in industrialized societies. If one Semai agrees to meet another so that they can undertake some joint activity, he will show up at the time agreed upon. Not do so would be "taboo" (*punan*). On the other hand, no one is tied to split-second accuracy. When they can afford it, the Semai like to buy wrist watches and clocks, but as ornaments rather than timepieces. Although someone in the minority of Semai who know how to read a dial might arrange to meet someone else at a given clock time, neither party would be upset if the other arrived half an hour early or late.

Similarly, the idea of a fixed routine is alien to Semai life. A Peace Corpsman told us about a Semai who worked for him on a road-building project. When the Semai showed up, he would arrive approximately on time. He would then work very hard and efficiently. In the course of a month he accomplished as much as his fellow workers, despite the fact that, on the two or three days a week when he had something else to do or simply did not feel like working, he would not come to work. Eventually, he was fired, not because he did less work than the Malays and Chinese on the road crew, but because his work pattern was different. The Semai tend to become restless under any system that inhibits their freedom of action or reduces their mobility. "It's as bad as having a wife," one man said of his job. In fact, as will become clear, the notion of a routine to which one's life must or should conform is not only strange to the Semai, it is also the sort of constraint which they say is likely to be bad for a person's health.

Because the Semai have a negative attitude toward routine, the following sketch of a Semai day is only statistically accurate. Some people in a settlement will probably be awake (or asleep) at any hour of the day or night. When someone is hungry, he does not wait until "mealtime"; he has a snack, whether it is the middle of the night or the middle of the afternoon. There is, moreover, a good deal of seasonal variation in daily routines. During fruit season, many people are likely to spend the whole day in the rain forest collecting fruit for sale or for domestic consumption. For instance, during July and August many people will spend a day or more in the rain forest collecting the oily nuts of the *pərah* (*Elateriospermum tapos*) or the foul-smelling but delectable beans of the *bətar* (*Parkia speciosa*). They will then sell these jungle products in the Chinese-Malay market, if there is one nearby, or to itinerant traders. In short, the account given below of a Semai day merely indicates the times when most people are most likely to be doing certain sorts of things.

The Semai do not divide their day into "morning," "afternoon," and "evening." Since their categories reflect the pattern of their life more accurately than English categories would, the following description divides the day the way the Semai do. The terms used are west Semai, but the east Semai categorization seems very similar.

HUPUR GƏGƏLAP "Dark *hupur*" begins at 4:30 or 5:00 A.M., before first light. The onset is marked by a change in the songs of the insects in the rain forest, as certain insects join the chorus and others fall silent. People begin to stir. Eventually someone gets up and kicks the fire into a glow. Some people grunt and roll over, pulling their sarongs over their heads to shut out the light. Others go to the hearth to stretch their arms and legs over the fire in order to drive away the damp chill of the night. (Nights on the hills can be quite cool. Although we used to sweat bucketfuls during the day, we always needed a light blanket at night.)

The people who are up and moving around pay little attention to those still asleep, except to avoid stepping over their bodies, an act that the Semai say might injure the sleeper's health. The general attitude seems to be that sleep is a purely private matter. No one would deliberately disturb a sleeper except for a matter of some urgency. On the other hand, no one is going to whisper or tiptoe around just because someone else is sleeping. Perhaps as a result of this attitude, the Semai seem able to sleep through a remarkable amount of noise. Visitors often went to sleep in our house while we were talking with other people, despite the sounds of conversation or typing.

Hupur gəgəlap, however, is a remarkably noisy time of day. Chicks begin cheeping, roosters crow, dogs yelp as someone throws them out of the house, cats squall as they are pulled from their places by the fire, people call out to their neighbors to see if they are awake or to invite them to share some tapioca. The people who are up shake out their sleeping mats, roll them up, and put them on the rafters or the floor by the wall. If they are hungry, they may scatter the cockroaches from the rice in last night's cooking pot. Babies are washed and fed. The result of all this noisy activity is that most people are awake by six or seven o'clock. Anyway, the Semai say, people who sleep later than that are likely to feel logy and depressed all day.

HUPUR By dawn most of the men and women who are going out to the field or the forest are on their way. Usually there are many who stay behind, but during planting season, most of the adults are out of the settlement before first light. Most of the people who leave before *hupur* do not wait for breakfast, although they may take along a piece of tapioca or some leftover rice in a bamboo tube. The idea is to get their activities over with before the day gets too hot, and the half hour required to cook tapioca or rice would cause too great a delay.

The people who stay behind are the ones who are sick, who plan to work indoors, or who have to face a day's work in the sun. In the last category would fall, for example, people who work on rubber plantations and women who have planned a basket-fishing expedition. They go out leisurely to defecate, usually accompanied by a neighbor or two. The women cook breakfast, usually tapioca or leftover rice and some side dish from the night before, if there is food left over. After a dip in the river, the people in the settlement go about their business. The women fill the household's bamboo tubes with water, wash clothes, weave mats or baskets, and pound rice. The men work on their blowpipes, make traps, collect firewood, split rattan, and so forth.

YAH   By ten or eleven o'clock most of the men who went hunting or fishing and most of the women who went to the fields for vegetables have returned to the settlement. If they have not already done so, they take a bath to cool off after their labor. This is one of the most eventful parts of the day. The men may have brought back a good catch, which is a topic of general interest and conversation. People who spent the morning apart exchange accounts of their experiences, often over the meal that everyone has about this time. After the meal, those who are tired may nap for an hour or so.

The closing hours of *yah* (about two or three o'clock) are the hottest, most humid, and most uncomfortable time of the day. A large part of the conversation at this time consists of complaints about the heat. On the other hand, one west Semai man said that "telling stories" during *yah* was likely to result in one's children's being born with "white eyes," that is, blind. Whatever the reason, people tend to be inactive in the early afternoon, and conversation tends to be desultory. From the Semai point of view, the end of *yah* marks the middle of the day in much the same way that noon marks the middle of the workday in some industrialized societies.

DUUI   By the beginning of *duui* people have finished eating and napping. This is the one time of day, according to some west Semai, that one should not sleep, because as the sun begins to set one's "soul" (*ruai*) may follow it, leaving one lethargic and depressed. Once again the population of the settlement splits up, some people staying at home and others going out into the rain forest. West Semai who have gathered rattan, wild banana leaves, or jungle fruits take their produce off to a nearby Chinese or Malay market for sale. These marketing groups are usually made up of men, since the women are too uneasy to deal effectively with non-Semai. The men may spend the rest of the afternoon in a coffee shop in town, spending what they have earned. They usually patronize only one shop, in part because they distrust the intentions of non-Semai too much to experiment with different shops. If the morning's fishing was good, the chances are that several fishing expeditions will set out in the afternoon. The women who have gone basket-fishing usually return shortly after the beginning of *duui,* at three or four o'clock.

As the day draws to a close, rain clouds frequently begin to gather. The rain itself usually starts late in the afternoon and continues into the evening. Sometimes it takes the form of a thundersquall, which frightens people, and which they propitiate ritually (see Chapter 2). More often it is simply a downpour, and some of the children strip off their clothes, if they are wearing any, and dance around under the cool raindrops.

By five or six o'clock most people are back home for the evening meal. My impression is that, since most of the hunting and fishing is done during *hupur,* the *duui* meal often consists of leftovers from the *yah* meal. Just before supper the women go to get water again. Afterwards, the adults sit around indoors or on the house ladders chatting about the day's events, while the children play outdoors.

KɔLɔM (MɔNGɔNT)   As darkness falls, visitors prepare to start back for their own houses, and the children go indoors. At the same time, especially if there has been a heavy rain, the fauna that live in the roof thatch—such as luminescent centipedes, brown and yellow tarantulas, small house rats—begin to emerge. The only really dangerous ones are some of the scorpions and the occasional giant centipede or venomous snake. The one the Semai like least is a tan cricket called *sɔment,* which people say is somehow associated with corpses and which they kill by holding its head in the fire.

With nightfall, Semai activities begin to cease. Most Semai households now have a small, funnel-shaped oil lamp, which furnishes a dim and flickering light. The oil is, in Semai terms, expensive, and people have to be rather chary with it. Most east Semai earn little or no money and must depend for lamp oil on trading with itinerant Malay or Chinese traders. Formerly, the Semai used bamboo tubes filled with resin as lamps, but most people have forgotten how to make them. At any rate, the artificial light available is not very adequate, and the onset of dusk is often the sign to go to sleep.

Although children can stay up as late as they like, most of them are asleep by about eight o'clock. Visitors have usually gone home by this time, since people are rather uneasy about being outdoors after dark. Their unease is justified. After nightfall, wild animals like the tiger already mentioned, sometimes enter a settlement. Besides wild animals, the Semai say, "gangsters," "evil spirits" (*nyani'*), and "death spirits" (*kɔtmoid*) are abroad at night. Shrill or twittering noises attract the "spirits." For this reason, after dark people should avoid whistling or playing the *pɔnsɔl,* a sort of flute played with the nose rather than the mouth.

MƏNGƆNT On an ordinary evening most adults are asleep by nine or ten o'clock. There is, however, some nighttime activity. A man and his wife may go out with torches to hunt grasshoppers or to fish. If a fishing expedition on a larger scale has been planned, it will probably take until nine or nine thirty to get it organized. By midnight the fishing parties have returned, and almost no one is awake.

Some evenings there is a ceremonial dance (the "sing" described in Chapter 9). "Sings" are held in a longhouse with a large central floor area on two or six successive nights. They provide an opportunity for boys and girls to flirt or to set a time later that night for the boy to sneak into the girl's house. There is no general obligation to attend a "sing," and groups of people drift in and out fairly freely, except when for ritual reasons the lights are put out and the door tied shut. By one o'clock in the morning most of the participants have gone home, although a couple of energetic men may keep on singing and dancing until *hupur gɔgɔlap.*

As the sounds of human activity subside, the sounds of the rain forest take over, a continuous susurration of insects, occasionally punctuated by the cough of a tiger or the shrill trumpeting of elephants. On moonlit nights there is also sometimes the sudden clatter of goats playing king of the castle on the house ladders. Against this background, one still often hears human noises, a man humming or singing himself to sleep, a sleepless woman playing the *kɔrib.* (The *kɔrib* is a piece of bamboo along which are strung two strands of palm fiber or rattan. To Euro-American ears the music of this two stringed lyre is haunting and melancholy, even when the tune is one called "Urinating in the River"). I was always moved by these small sounds against the vast, inhuman chirring of the rain forest. They seemed like an assertion of Semai humanity in a world where both nature and society were indifferent to whether or not the Semai survived.

The Nonviolent Image and *Punan*

CHAPTER 5 INTRODUCED the word *punan,* translating it as a sort of "taboo" that keeps people from breaking the rules of food distribution. The concept of *punan,* however, is more complex than the word "taboo" indicates, although the word in both English and Semai probably comes from a Malayo-Polynesian word like *tapu.* Since the concept of *punan* pervades Semai ideas about interpersonal relationships, a clear understanding of it is essential to understanding how the Semai get along together.

Implicit in Semai thinking about *punan* is the idea that to make someone unhappy, especially by frustrating his desires, will increase the probability of his having an accident that will injure him physically. The word *punan* refers to both the offending act and the resulting accident proneness. The Semai say that *punan* accidents result somehow from the fact that the *punan* victim's heart is "unhappy." A Semai who has had an accident, like barking his shin, will often blame the accident on *punan,* due, for example, to his wanting something he could not get.

The function of *punan* as a sanction that enforces "proper" behavior in social relationships depends on a translation of intangible offenses, like not providing food on request, into a kind of violence that may inflict physical harm on the victim, like a broken leg. The offense and the accident proneness are bracketed together by the single word *punan.* For this sanction to work, then, it must be postulated that the Semai are not the sort of people who would do each other physical harm. After all, a punishment that afflicts the victim rather than the offender is unlikely to deter the latter if he is unscrupulous.

It is, therefore, not surprising that the Semai attribute to themselves the characteristics necessary for *punan* to work as a sanction. The Semai conceive of themselves as nonviolent people, and each Semai tends to think of himself as a nonviolent person. For purposes of brevity I will refer to this collective self-image as the "nonviolent image." This image is not merely an ideal to strive for. The Semai do not say, "Anger is bad." They say, "We do not get angry," and an obviously angry man will flatly deny his anger. The Semai do not say, "It is forbidden to hit

55

people." They say, "We do not hit people." The point here is not that sometimes individual Semai violate the nonviolent image, for they do, being human. It is, rather, that they contine to conceive of themselves as nonviolent. Without some such concept of "human nature" in its Semai form the effectiveness of *punan* as a sanction would be lost.

This nonviolent image is the face the Semai present to the outside world. They are famous in Malaya for their timidity. British observers who have spent little time with the Semai inevitably use adjectives like "timid" or "weak" to describe them. Those who have spent a few weeks with the Semai usually see them as "carefree" or "jolly." Almost never does one run across the words so common in European travelers' descriptions of "natives": surly, hostile, insolent.

The questions posed in this chapter, then, are these. How do the Semai manage to keep the nonviolent image plausible? And what are the repercussions of this crucial image in Semai life?

Expressing Hostility

Despite the claim that "we never get angry," Semai do, of course, sometimes quarrel and harbor ill will against each other. Say that one man refuses the legitimate request of another, thus putting him into *punan*. There are two courses of action immediately open to the victim. He may simply endure the *punan*, or he may go to the offender and ask compensation.

Enduring *punan* is commonest when a girl has refused the victim her sexual favors. The jilted man's "heart becomes sad." He loses his energy and his appetite. Much of the time he sleeps, dreaming of his lost love. In this state he is in fact very likely to injure himself "accidentally."

In most other instances the victim seeks compensation from the wrongdoer. The wronged person or a kinsman acting as his intermediary goes to the guilty party and explains the situation: he has made so-and-so unhappy, put him in *punan*. To reverse this situation, the offender must apologize and pay a fine so that the victim's heart will be happy again. In the east the matter must be settled on a purely personal level. The amount of compensation demanded is proportionate to the amount of emotional distress the offense has caused. For instance, if one person has "embarrassed" another, the amount of compensation varies depending on just how "embarrassed" the victim was. No abstract concept of justice is involved. There are two main ways of collecting compensation. The first is for the victim to set a fine, often far beyond the offender's ability to pay. Then he or a kinsman acting for him discuss the amount of compensation with the offender. In the course of this discussion the two parties decide on the minimum gift that will make the victim happy again and repair the ties of amity between offender and victim. Frequently the gift of a fairly small item like a cooking pot is enough to restore harmony. The second way of getting compensation, say the Semai, is the "smarter" way. If the victim thinks the offender unlikely to pay compensation voluntarily, he may keep his grievance to himself and bide his time until the unwary offender presents him with an opportunity to pre-empt compensation. He might, for example, take the clothes the offender has left ashore while bathing. When the offender comes ashore, the victim explains that he has collected compensation for such-and-such an act. Knowing his own guilt, the offender is unlikely to put up much of an argument.

The west Semai have adopted the Malay system of a set schedule of fines for various offenses. Again, however, the parties negotiate, and the settlement is usually less than the official standard.

If both parties feel in the right, however, these negotiations may not lead to reconciliation. A possible next step is to appeal to respected elders in the community to adjudicate the dispute. In the east, however, there is no particular social pressure to seek such advice. Besides, east Semai settlements are often so small that all the elders are related to one or the other of the disputants and thus unable to give a disinterested judgment. If one of the quarrelers thinks the judgment is unjust, moreover, he is free to ignore it. Rejecting the elders' decision may embroil him in a quarrel with them as well, but they have no way to enforce their decision. Similarly, west Semai may refuse to ask the elders to resolve a dispute, in part because both parties can be fined for breach of the peace, a Malay-style concept unknown to the east Semai. If the elders are brought in, their decision is morally binding on the disputants. Nevertheless, there is no way of enforcing it, although public opinion will favor conforming to it. In short, most quarrels are conceived of as personal matters, and the social institutions for resolving quarrels are rather ineffective.

Perhaps for this reason, quarrelers rarely try to get disinterested parties to mediate a dispute. They try to involve other people, but as partisans rather than mediators. They usually spread unsavory rumors about each other, protesting at the same time that they themselves are not angry and would like nothing better than to settle the dispute by peaceful discussion. For example, a man will describe how he tried to talk to the person with whom he is quarreling. In such descriptions, the other party invariably refuses to talk things over, saying, "I'm not listening to you," and typically threatening the narrator with a weapon. It is hard to gauge the truth of these stories, all of which are embroidered to support the narrator's case. Besides spreading rumors behind each other's backs, they manifest their anger not in violence but in mutual avoidance. Should the disputants happen to meet, they pay no attention to each other. Each is too "embarrassed" to look directly at the other. Eventually, one or the other will move off to a new settlement.

Once in a while, when a quarrel is just beginning, people will call each other names and make threatening gestures at each other. The names are epithets like "you cockroach" rather than curses. Sometimes a very angry person will start throwing his property around without hurting anyone. The Semai say that such outbursts are "not good" because they "scare" people. They seem to be uncommon.

More direct expression of aggression is very rare. For example, one might expect that a drunken Semai would show the startling transformation that sometimes occurs in Euro-American society when a normally meek person gets drunk and becomes violent. Although aboriginally the Semai had no alcoholic drinks, now west Semai men can buy beer or a kind of palm wine called toddy. Sometimes on a special occasion like the visit of a beloved but rarely seen relative, a man will drink enough to get noticeably drunk. Drunk, he becomes extremely talkative, noisier than usual, but apparently never violent.

Similarly, although the often heard statement that "we never hit our children" is primarily lip service to the nonviolent image, people do not often hit their children and almost never administer the kind of beating that is routine in some sectors of Euro-American society. A person should never hit a child because, people say, "How would you feel if it died?" Malays, say the Semai, "are always hitting, hitting, hitting their children." Semai almost never do. That is why, they conclude, Semai children are healthy and fat while Malay children are whining and scrawny, "like baby rats." Similarly, one adult should never hit another because, they say, "Suppose he hit you back?" Some idea of the horror that physical violence inspires in Semai is revealed by the fact that when east Semai are talking Malay they translate the Semai word for "hit" as "kill."

As noted in Chapter 3, the Semai are uneasy about killing animals, especially those they have raised themselves. If a person must kill a chicken, for example, he saws the head off rather than chop it off, because he "can't stand hearing that 'thunk.'" Murder, of course, is almost unthinkable. Informants said there were no penalties for murder because "it never happens, in the olden days or today." Since a census of the Semai was first taken in 1956, not one instance of murder, attempted murder, or maiming has come to the attention of either government or hospital authorities.

The Semai do, however, make an exception for one sort of nonviolent killing. In the old days during times of scarcity the Semai would reluctantly abandon very old or hopelessly sick people, who were completely unproductive, in a hut with a small supply of food and water to die. The only documented instance of such abandonment occurred in 1956 when the Communist uprising had reduced all the Semai to dire economic straits. The Semai are uneasy about such abandonment. They say that they never go near the spot where someone was abandoned. But they insist that abandonment is not really "killing" and that the abandoned person is usually in such misery that he or she wants to die. Some people, of course, deny that such an apparent contravention of the nonviolent image occurs.

It should be clear at this point that the Semai are not great warriors. As long as they have been known to the outside world, they have consistently fled rather than fight, or even than run the risk of fighting. They had never participated in a war or raid until the Communist insurgency of the early 1950s, when the British raised troops among the Semai, mainly in the west. Initially, most of the recruits were probably lured by wages, pretty clothes, shotguns, and so forth. Many did not realize that soldiers kill people. When I suggested to one east Semai recruit that killing was a soldier's job, he laughed at my ignorance and explained, "No, we don't kill people, brother, we just tend weeds and cut grass." Apparently, he had up to that point done nothing but grounds duty.

Many people who knew the Semai insisted that such an unwarlike people could never make good soldiers. Interestingly enough, they were wrong. Communist terrorists had killed the kinsmen of some of the Semai counterinsurgency troops. Taken out of their nonviolent society and ordered to kill, they seem to have been swept up in a sort of insanity which they call "blood drunkenness." A typical veteran's story runs like this. "We killed, killed, killed. The Malays would stop and go through people's pockets and take their watches and money. We did not think of watches or money. We thought only of killing. Wah, truly we were drunk with blood." One man even told how he had drunk the blood of a man he had killed.

Talking about these experiences, the Semai seem bemused, not displeased that they were such good soldiers, but unable to account for their behavior. It is almost as if they had shut the experience off in a separate compartment, away from the even routine of their lives. Back in Semai society they seem as gentle and afraid of violence as anyone else. To them their one burst of violence appears to be as remote as something that happened to someone else, in another country. The nonviolent image remains intact.

In brief, little violence occurs within Semai society. Violence, in fact, seems to terrify the Semai. A Semai does not meet force with force, but with passivity or flight. Yet, he has no institutionalized way of preventing violence—no social controls, no police or courts. Somehow a Semai learns automatically always to keep tight rein over his aggressive impulses. Given the weakness of external controls, the Semai need internal ones. The learning process involved is the subject of the next section of this chapter.

Enculturation

TRAINING TECHNIQUES   The Semai, especially the east Semai, emphatically deny that they teach their children. They tend to equate teaching with the child-beating which they rather inaccurately attribute to Malays. "Our children just learn by themselves," they say. The physical punishment meted out to children usually consists merely of pinching the cheek lightly, or patting the hands.

In fact, Semai children do have considerable freedom. The word *bood* means, roughly, "not to feel like doing something." If a parent tells a child to do something and the child replies, "I *bood*," the matter is closed. To put pressure on the child is *punan*. Furthermore, although an adult may suggest that a child watch how something is done, children learn most adult activities by imitative play that gradually becomes adult work. For instance, at planting time a little girl toddles off to the fields with her mother or grandmother, playfully digs a few holes, and stuffs tapioca stalks into them. Each year as she gets older she plants more tapioca until by the time she is in her teens she is planting as much as her mother. Most Semai children's games are small-scale rehearsals of adult activity, although in the west some games imitate activities seen in the movies. One east Semai game is especially interesting because it seems to be a sort of symbolic rehearsal for refraining from violence. In this game children of both sexes from two- to ten-year-olds flail away wildly at each other with long sticks, assuming dramatically aggressive postures. Yet the sticks always freeze inches away from the target, and although it seems inevitable that someone will be hit by mistake, no one ever is. Similarly, the usual pattern of play wrestling is to throw the opponent almost but not quite to the ground. Again, no one gets hurt even when, as is often the case, one child is much bigger than the other. Incidentally, there seem to be no indigenous games that involve competition.

The Semai indulge their babies. Since infants cannot talk, the Semai say, they cannot understand, and there is no sense trying to discipline them. Consequently, an infant can do almost anything it wants—hit people, expose its genitals, defecate anywhere, upset household arrangements. Everyone cuddles, carries, and plays with it. If it weeps, someone is always on hand to comfort it or to divert its attention. It sleeps between its parents, so that either can get up and rock it if it wakes up and weeps.

The Semai say correctly that once a child has learned to walk and talk it is likely to survive. It is also less fun to play with. When a child cries in the settlement, parents look out of their houses to see if it is their child. If not, they return to what they were doing, letting the child cry itself out or make its own way home. Moreover, if a child cannot explain what has made it cry, or if there is nothing to do about it, even the child's own parents let it cry unattended. In short, the coddling world of infancy abruptly becomes relatively cold and uncaring.

Moreover, many Semai (especially in the east) feel that children are inherently "naughty" (*duus*) because they have not learned to refrain from improper activities. The child therefore has to be "scared" (*sarangɔh*) out of doing bad or dangerous things. An irate parent may shout at a child, "I'm going to hit you!" and make as if to hit the child with his hand, a machete, a burning piece of bamboo, or the like. But, as in the children's game described above, the blow freezes inches from its target, and the worst the child usually gets is a tap. More commonly, parents will try to scare a child with threats. People shout "Fear! Fall! Fall!" at children climbing trees. A child may be threatened with evil spirits (*nyani'*). If it interrupts a conversation of its elders, it is told that its genitals will swell to enormous size. Two of the commonest bugaboos used to scare children are *mai* and *talaid*.

Children learn to fear strangers (*mai*). Whenever we first visited a settlement, people took the opportunity to scare their children. "The Pale People have come to stick you with hypodermics," they might say, "Who is most afraid? Point him out! That's the one we're going to stick first." Some people used our presence as a chance to frighten children of both strangers and evil spirits (*nyani'*). "See the *nyani'*," a mother might say, pointing to us. "Fear! Fear! They're going to eat you! Fear! Fear!" The adults are amused, the children frightened. Later on the parents can use the learned fear of *mai* and *nyani'* to scare the children in other situations.

The idea of *talaid* discussed in Chapter 2, is most highly developed among the east Semai and their Semang neighbors, although it is also found in the west. If east Semai children tease defenseless creatures or make too much noise at play the settlement rings with cries of *"Tarlaid Tarlaid!"* A Semai child can see how frightened adults are of thundersqualls. During a storm, the adults cry, "Fear! Fear!" to the children and urge them to cover their eyes against the lightning and their ears against the thunder. The adults thus increase the children's own fears of the violence of nature. The next time the children seem to be becoming noisy and potentially losing their self-control, the cry of *"Tarlaid!"* recalls to them the terrifying thundersquall and subtly suggests to them that the expression of human violence would be as devastating as the storm. The children in this way apparently learn to fear their own aggressive impulses.

All this does not mean that a Semai child lives in an atmosphere of terror. To be sure, he learns to fear the potential violence of others and the results of any expression of his own aggressive impulses. But the fear can be handled. Faced with others' violence he can always flee. And he can learn to control his own hostile feelings to the point where he can say, "I never get angry," and believe it. Thus he gains the ability to avert the threatened dangers. Besides, most of the time adults are too busy with their own affairs to be continually threatening children. The child is left to his own devices and learns to rely on himself and his self-control. This general self-control both reinforces and is reinforced by the concept of oneself as a Semai, a nonviolent person.

AGGRESSION TRAINING Besides the inculcation of self-control by threats, there are two other factors that apparently make Semai children tend to conform to the nonviolent image. The first, paradoxically, is that the Semai do not deliberately punish aggression in children. Young children sometimes try to hit adults, but are fended off with laughter or a threat. The only aggression the children usually see are the abortive hitting gestures that they imitate in their games. They thus have little personal experience with human violence, except that they may be taught that human violence and the violence of a thundersquall are similar. Moreover, they cannot rebel against their parents because the parents do not object when the child bood, that is, refuses to do something because it "doesn't feel like it." The absence of punishment means that the would-be aggressive child has no model to imitate and that, not knowing for sure what the results of human violence are, he winds up with an exaggerated impression of them.

The second factor that seems to keep Semai children from becoming violent is the low permissiveness adults accord fighting among children. It will be remembered that the nonviolent image is stated not merely as an ideal but also as a fact. The Semai expect that their children will conform to the image. Children become aware of this expectation as it is manifested both in subtle daily ways and in the open shock of adults when a child loses its temper. In the latter case, an adult immediately snatches up the angry child and carries it off wailing to its house. This abrupt intervention is probably all the more frightening because adults usually are indifferent to children's activities.

Ramifications of the Nonviolent Image

SEX AND AGGRESSION The Semai word *sumbung* seems to come from two Malay words, *sombong* and *sumbang*. *Sombong* means roughly "uppity and arrogant." For example, a Semai child who interrupts his elders is *sombong*. To be *sombong* is to violate the nonviolent image. *Sumbang,* on the other hand, refers to sexual offenses, especially incest. The Semai word *sumbung* embraces the meanings of both these Malay words. Thus, a Semai child who interrupts his elders is not merely aggressive but also in some sense sexually out of line.

It is reasonable in this context to threaten a disrespectful child that its genitals will swell to enormous size because an aggressive breach of propriety falls into the same category as sexual misbehavior. Conversely, sexual misbehavior logically is *tɔrlaid,* like any other action that is considered violent. For instance, the Semai interpret a dream of a snake indoors to mean that someone in the dreamer's settlement harbors incestuous desires, but a dream of a snake outdoors is said to predict a thundersquall. This equation of sexual and aggressive behavior as *sumbung* complicates Semai sexual affairs.

For example, the usual pattern of initiating sexual contact is for the man to wheedle the woman into lying on her back with her knees raised so that he may sit between her legs and copulate with her. This wheedling can easily shade off into nagging. A woman may say that she got married simply because her husband was always nagging her, and he will admit, "That's right, I was crazy about her." The problem here is that refusing a request is *punan*. Unwilling people will sometimes yield to prolonged nagging. Since the consent is unwilling, however, such prolonged nagging is also *punan*, simultaneously sexual and aggressive. The east Semai say that nagging or threatening a person into yielding to one's sexual advances is the same as raping her.

To a casual observer the east Semai seem to be freer about sexual relations than the west Semai. For example, the east Semai are more casual about the sexual activities of children, who sometimes play overt sexual games. A boy may, for instance, pretend to copulate with a girl, using a corncob as a penis, while watching adults whoop with laughter. Adolescent boys often expose the genitals of younger boys as a joke, for example, by lifting them out of the water while bathing. On the other hand, as soon as a west Semai child can speak a few words, its kinsmen begin to put its hands over its genitals, saying "Cover up! Cover up! Be embarrassed!" They pat its hand away when it plays with itself and rebuke it for talking about sex, often threatening that its genitals will swell.

Similarly, the east Semai expect there to be a good deal of premarital and extramarital sexual activity. The west Semai have taken over the Malay code that limits sexual activity, although the rules are often ignored. The relative nudity of the east Semai was contrasted with west Semai clothing style in Chapter 2.

With respect to breasts it is worth noting that, although east Semai men and women display a marked overt interest in plump breasts and call any rounded protuberance on an artifact its "breast," nevertheless their interest seems to be more in suckling than in overt sexual activity. This interest may be connected with the fact that east Semai children are allowed to suckle much longer than their west Semai counterparts. In the east children start getting prechewed foods when they are about a year old. People say that an infant given solid food too early will grow up a glutton. If a child has no younger brothers or sisters, he may suckle for nourishment until he is four or five years old. If he has a younger brother or sister, or if he is over six years old, he usually has to ask repeatedly for the breast before he can suckle. Such occasional suckling goes on until the child nears puberty. Weaning is gradual, typically initiated by offering the child substitutes for the breast, like food or cigarettes. Instead of sucking their thumbs most east Semai children smoke, and it is not unusual to see a child a year or two old take a puff on a cigarette after having finished suckling at his mother's breast. West Semai children, on the other hand, are usually weaned by the age of two. The method of weaning is the same as in the east, but commercial pacifiers are substituted for cigarettes. Probably the west Semai cover their breasts more in imitation of Malays than because the breasts are sexually attractive to men. For both the east and west Semai the focus of sexual interest is on the genitals. The genitals are the only part of the body adults consistently keep covered, even from members of the same sex. When bathing, for example, the Semai keep their hands over their genitals until they are submerged. No one uses the words for the genitals in polite conversation.

Despite the fact that the east Semai apparently have a freer sex life, the explicit equation of certain sorts of sexual misbehavior with violence seems to disturb them more than it disturbs the west Semai. East Semai often talk about their first sexual experience as if it had been very frightening. They say that even after a virgin boy or girl has consented it may take weeks to consummate the relationship because the inexperienced person is so scared. As one man said of his reluctance to copulate with his first woman, "Her vagina looked like a house to me, a *big* house." East Semai women are so afraid of being raped "by Malays" that they will not sleep alone in a house even when there are no Malays for miles around. West Semai women seem to worry somewhat less about rape.

Finally, the Semai report a type of behavior rather like Malay *latah*. This reported behavior system, said to occur chiefly among older women, involves spells during which the victim compulsively repeats whatever is said to her (echolalia) and compulsively mimics any actions she sees (echopraxia). Any startling event may set off these echo reactions. The west Semai speak of them not as symptoms of an underlying insanity but as an amusing personal idiosyncrasy so much like stammering that the same word serves for both. They sometimes good naturedly try to startle the woman into echo reactions by suddenly shouting the Semai equivalent of "Boo!" at her. When the east Semai talk about this behavior system, even when referring to actual cases, they almost always claim that the victim also shouts sexual obscenities and exposes her genitals. The point here is not that east Semai mental disorders always involve sexual misbehavior. For that I have no evidence. The point is that the east Semai expect sexual misbehavior to occur when other aberrant behavior occurs, whereas the west Semai do not.

NONINTERFERENCE   The word *pərsusah* comes from the root *susah*, "difficult, unhappy." To *pərsusah* someone is thus to make difficulties for him and/or to make him unhappy. Such actions are, of course, *punan*. A phrase that crops up regularly when one Semai speaks well of another is "He doesn't *pərsusah* people." Similarly, a Semai community will cheerfully tolerate a person who by Euro-American standards is insane or hopelessly retarded as long as he does not *pərsusah* people.

The Semai extend the word *pərsusah* to cover almost any kind of unsolicited meddling in the affairs of others. In fact, the phrase "the affairs of others" (*hal mai*) is used to indicate that the speaker has no rights and duties in the matter and therefore finds talking about it a waste of time and a bore. Noninterference in "the affairs of others" is an integral part of the nonviolent image.

Conversely, when "others" interfere in one's own affairs, the prescribed response is withdrawal or passivity. For example, we several times heard almost identical stories about how Malays set upon a friend of the narrator. The friend fled, but the narrator blocked the Malays' pursuit, spreading his arms and saying, "Kill me, but let my friend go." This response allegedly shamed the Malays out of their aggression. The truth of these stories is not important. The significant thing is that this is the way the narrator would like to act and perhaps the way he thinks he would act. It is the course of action most consonant with the nonviolent image.

This principle of noninterference seems to give rise to a feeling that human relationships are insecure in the sense that one is always essentially alone. *Sɔra'ngiid sɔngiid luui,* is an east Semai proverb. The literal meaning is "thinking thinks by itself." The sense is that the thoughts of the heart only the heart can know. "You cannot know my grief," says a west Semai man. "You feel grief, but not the real grief. For you it *must* always be like a movie." An extension of this feeling is the general opinion that sympathy is "useless." "What good does it do an unhappy person to have another person upset?" people ask.

The abrupt change from the world of infancy to that of childhood may possibly exacerbate this explicit sense of the individual's essential aloneness. Just as the break comes, the mother is likely to be pregnant again. To the shock of the transition into childhood is added the shock of realizing that a new infant is likely to take the child's place. At this time, say the Semai, children are likely to be withdrawn or even to fall sick. They often observably turn away from their pregnant mother and lavish their affections on other members of the household, a father or grandparent. They begin to have dreams of the sort that in Euro-Americans would indicate insecurity, for example, dreams of falling. The midwife who delivered a child and is therefore supposed to be emotionally very close to it should be especially alert about the child's welfare when a younger sibling[1] is born.

To make matters more difficult for the child, it is usually given some of the responsibility for looking after the baby. The child often seems to express its hostility toward the infant by so smothering it with "affection" that the baby cries and tries to get away. More direct expression of aggression would, of course, be impossible. The parents laugh when the infant hits the older child but immediately rebuke any retaliation. The upshot is that there seems to be an undercurrent of indirectly expressed fear and resentment of young brothers and sisters.

This feeling makes itself evident in indirect ways. For instance, the Semai say that the younger of two brothers will be the larger, although in fact the opposite is true. A small species of catfish is called the "elder brother" of the giant catfish. Similarly, in Semai stories the younger brothers or sisters are luckier than the older ones and also often treat the older ones badly, as in the tale of Enku (see Chapter 2).

---

[1] Brother or sister.

7

The Problem of Authority

TO GIVE ORDERS or to try to make others do something they do not want to do is to *pɔrsusah* them. Arrogating to oneself the authority to do so is *sumbung*. Seeking authority is not consonant with the nonviolent image. For example, a west Semai man who seemed to be actively undermining the headman's prestige and extending his own influence repeatedly denied that he had any desire to become headman himself. Even parents, it will be remembered, do not have the authority to make their children do something the children "do not feel like" doing. Authority is thus a prickly problem in Semai society. The way the Semai deal with this problem is discussed in this chapter.

Elders

There are two major reasons for the importance of age in Semai social organization. The first is that in a society with no written tradition and little oral tradition wisdom consists largely of the lifelong accumulation of personal experience. The older a Semai is, the more he knows and the greater his expertise at dealing with his fellows. Such wisdom merits respect. Second, for reasons discussed in Chapter 8, young people and young married couples frequently move around from settlement to settlement. Eventually, however, they settle down in one place. It is therefore the older, settled married couples who supply stability and continuity to a Semai settlement or large household. By virtue of this position they win the respect of the younger people.

At first it seems as if Semai communities are run by a council of elders. There is in fact a Semai word for "elder" (*rana'*) which comes from the same root as the word for "old" (*ɔnra'*). The elders have no authority to enforce their decisions, however, and the variety of ways in which the Semai calculate age often makes it hard to tell just who the elders are.

The fact that the Semai respect the elders does not mean that they have to obey them, any more than a child has to obey his parent if he *bood*. A Semai takes heed of what his elders say. In the Semai phrase, he "hears" them. He does not interrupt when they are speaking, nor does he address them familiarly. No Semai, for example, would talk about sex to someone in his father's generation. On the other hand, after listening respectfully to them, he may reject their advice. If they press the point, he may say, "I don't hear you." Although a senior may have great influence over some of his juniors, he cannot order them to do anything they do not want to do.

The Semai calculate age in three rather different ways. The first is chronological age. The Semai are vague about measurements—the aboriginal counting system goes "one, two, three, many"—and people guess rather wildly at how old they are. For example, an east Semai about thirty years old may estimate his age as eighty or a hundred. They do recognize certain physical indicators of age. A "new child" or infant cannot walk or talk. A "child" has no secondary sexual characteristics. An "adolescent" has recently reached sexual maturity. An adult (no Semai word) is a person between adolescence and old age. An "oldster" has white hair, wrinkled breasts, et cetera.

Another way of calculating age is on the basis of childbearing. A "child" has no children and is not mature enough to have any. An "adolescent" could bear children but has not done so. An adult can and does have children. An "oldster" has children but can no longer bear them. This method of calculating age is closely related to the Semai system of names. A "child" gets his real name (*muh*) as the result of his position in the birth order, for example, "First-born" (Long), "Second-born" (Alang), and so forth. When he is old enough to talk, he also gets a nickname (*mɔl,* "handle") which is based on the first word he speaks or on some personal characteristic (for example, "Stinky" or "Noisy"). When he becomes an adolescent, his childhood nickname comes to "embarrass" him and, especially if he moves to a new settlement, he takes or is given a new one. Next, when a woman becomes pregnant for the first time, she and her husband take new names meaning "Father/Mother Pregnant." When the child is born, these names change to "Father/Mother of Boy/Girl." After the child is old enough to get a nickname, people begin to call the parents "Father/Mother of So-and-So." Anthropologists call the custom whereby a parent takes his child's name "teknonymy," and the names themselves are "teknonyms." Parents continue to use these new names unless the child dies, in which case they use the name of the next eldest child if any, or revert to using their own names. People who are sterile are called "Father/Mother of Sterility." Finally, when a person passes the age of childbearing, he may be called "Grampa/Gramma So-and-So," using his own name, his teknonym, or his grandchild's name.

The third sort of age which is important to the Semai is relative age. A Semai child classifies a large portion of the people he knows as "old people" to whom, as noted in Chapter 6, he has to defer if he doesn't want his genitals to swell hugely. Conversely, an old Semai calls more people "children" or "adolescents" than his younger associates would. Consequently, a person may find that men much his elder refer to him still in a patronizing and familiar way by his name or nickname, while men much his junior refer to him respectfully by his teknonym.

The reason for spending so much space on how the Semai reckon age is that having these three types of calculations lets the individual Semai emphasize familiarity or respect pretty much as he wishes. The absence of a specific term for "adult" has much the same effect, since a person can classify his associates as "adolescents" or "oldsters" depending on the kind of relationship he wants to have with them. In an argument between two influential men, the elder may refer to the younger contemptuously as an "adolescent," even though the younger is both biologically and chronologically adult. Similarly, a person who esteems the wisdom of another may call him "Grampa." Thus, the Semai refer to the young, childless, and dedicated head of the medical staff of the Department of Aborigines as "Grampa Bolton." The result is that a Semai does not become an "elder" simply by growing old. He has somehow to gain the respect of the other people in his settlement. Otherwise people will not recognize his claims to be an elder and may even keep on using his name instead of his teknonym. The flexibility of the Semai system of reckoning age is reflected in the difficulty of getting informants to agree just who the elders in a community are. There is some agreement about universally respected elders, but after giving those names people add different names according to their personal preferences.

In short, a Semai should respect the aged. The rules for calculating who is an "elder," however, are so flexible that a person has considerable leeway in deciding just whom he wants to respect.

Headmen

Community leadership provides a fine example of the sort of misunderstanding that has occurred between the Semai and their non-Semai neighbors. In the old days, a settlement had no formal leaders, although there were influential elders who could sometimes persuade people to follow their suggestions. The office of headman is a new one, inadvertently created by non-Semai to serve their own interests. With the cessation of the slave trade the Semai came to have more and more peaceful contacts with non-Semai, especially in the west, where non-Semai were far more numerous. To handle such contacts the Semai relied on one of the elders who could speak Malay and who was brave enough to deal with *mai* (non-Semai). The non-Semai misunderstood this man's position in the settlement, thinking of him as if he were a Malay headman. They called him "headman" and treated him as if he had some authority over the people for whom he was the spokesman. At first, of course, he had no such authority.

At the turn of the century the Sultan of Perak began to assert Malay authority over the Semai by giving certain west Semai elders fancy titles and "letters of authority" (*surat kuasa*) that acknowledged them as "headmen." During the Communist insurgency in the early 1950s the British extended this system to the east Semai in hopes of gaining control over them. The first trained anthropologist to study the Senoi-speaking peoples, the late Pat Noone, had a low opinion of the *surat kuasa*. "It is," he wrote in an unpublished report to the government, "merely a makeshift piece of paper designed to delude the Sakai [Semai] into thinking that they are secure." For the east Semai, however, these letters have taken on a magical potency as talismans against the possible malevolence of non-Semai. The result is that the influence of the elder given a *surat kuasa* has increased, while the influence on the other elders has declined. People now say, "I don't hear you, you have no *surat*," and a headman relies heavily on his *surat* to assert his authority.

Even with a *surat*, a Semai headman is merely the most senior, in terms of prestige, of a group of influential men, not an autocrat. He keeps the peace by conciliation rather than coercion. He must be personally respected as well as having a *surat*. Otherwise people will drift away from him or gradually stop paying attention to him. Moreover, the Semai recognize only two or three occasions on which he can assert his authority: dealing as a representative of his people with non-Semai; mediating a quarrel, if invited by the quarreling parties to do so but not otherwise; and, in the west, selecting and apportioning land for fields. On all other occasions he has no more authority than any other elder. Furthermore, most of the time a good headman gauges the general feeling about an issue and bases his decision on that, so that he is more a spokesman for public opinion than a molder of it.

In short, although outsiders have introduced a position of authority into the Semai band, the authority itself is diluted, and a Semai can ignore it entirely by moving to another band or settlement. The ability of one person to constrain the actions of another is limited.

Public Opinion

In societies where there is little authority and few constraining rules public opinion becomes of great importance. It takes the place of authority or rules in validating one person's claims against another's, in letting someone know whether he is doing the right thing. A Semai who can win public opinion to his side can usually get things done. He wins public opinion by using certain techniques of persuasion. Understanding these techniques is therefore of prime importance in understanding Semai society.

In general, older men wield the greatest influence over public opinion. As already noted, age and wisdom tend to be associated with each other in Semai society. No rule prevents women from being influential, and some women are. Most of the time, however, Semai women are primarily concerned with the petty affairs of hearth and home. As a Semai proverb puts it, "Men's loincloths are long, women's loincloths are short," that is, men are concerned with major problems, women with minor ones. Furthermore, Semai women feel "embarrassed" to take a prominent part in public debate, although a woman often exercises influence through her husband. For example, prophetic dreams are a sign of wisdom, and gossip has it that one headman routinely presents his wife's dreams as his own.

A Semai is most likely to persuade his kinsmen to side with him in a quarrel or to cooperate with him in some activity. Other people, who are *mai* (in the sense of "nonkinsmen") to him and to whom he is *mai*, are less likely to help him. Not only are his kinsmen more likely than others to help him, they are more ready to heed his advice and to treat him with respect. One of the reasons it is impossible to talk about a "council of elders" in Semai society is that informants are so prejudiced in favor of their kinsmen that they label them "elders" when *mai* do not. When a person is trying to win public support for his side in a dispute, his kinsmen will usually join him in spreading his side of the story, often adding unsavory rumors about his opponent. In short, a man with many kinsmen in a given settlement is more likely to win arguments and to get things done his way than a man with few kismen is.

A second way of influencing public opinion is by verbal facility. Almost all influential Semai are good public speakers. Debating techniques include the use of irony, specifics and proverbs rather than generalities, organization of material by numbered topic, simile, metaphor, rhetorical questions, and a sprinkling of jokes. At the same time, an experienced public speaker will make fun of an opponent's proposal, or he may make a witty aside to the audience while his opponent is speaking seriously.

The Semai enjoy good debates, greeting telling points with cries of "Hear! Hear!" In fact, some east Semai seem to feel that a well-stated assertion not refuted by fact is almost necessarily true. For instance, I finished the story of Samson and Delilah (transmuted into a Semai and a Malay, respectively) with the usual Semai disavowal: "A tale of the old ones—I don't know if it's true." The audience responded fervently, "Oh, it *must* be true, it *must* be true." Similarly, a good metaphor may clinch an argument. For instance, a west Semai defended his daughter's returning home without first consulting her in-laws. Her half-Chinese husband had hit her, he said, and "my child isn't a water buffalo." People discussing the affair always quoted this remark, which was important in turning public opinion against the husband.

Because verbal facility can be used to pressure people, however, the Semai regard it with suspicion. On the one hand, verbal facility is taken as a sign of intelligence. People who are not fluent are *kalɔɔ,* "dumb" in the twofold sense of unspeaking and stupid. They are not influential, whatever their age or kinship ties. On the other hand, they are less dangerous then fluent speakers. By analogy nonvenomous snakes and stingless bees are the "dumb" ones. The Semai speaker must be careful not to press his point too hard. He must be bold enough to speak out forcefully, but he cannot be too forceful. If his audience feels he is putting pressure on them, they will become resentful and uncooperative. Self-deprecation is therefore an important rhetorical trick, and most speeches begin with a phrase like "I'm getting old and deaf, but . . ."

Other things being equal, popularity is an important way of gaining influence over public opinion. The man who shares what he can afford without seeming to calculate his expenditure is likely to be popular. Such generosity means that his wife must be generous, too, so that she doesn't try to stint his giving. Many people will then call at his house and listen to what he has to say, a prime index of influence.

The popular man like the fluent speaker must play down his influence. He may refer to it indirectly, for example, "More people visit me than visit the headman." He must not seem to seek power over others, however, nor to enjoy bossing them, or people will say, "His heart is big." Having the reputation of a big (that is, *sumbung*) heart is a sure way of losing influence.

In brief, public opinion is the main external constraint on individual activities. The Semai say, "There is no authority here but embarrassment." When public opinion goes against him, a Semai is "embarrassed." Even so, with the proper skills he is able to manipulate the consensus. An older man can gain influence by having many kinsmen, by verbal facility, and by personal popularity. He must, however, always keep his realization that he is influential to himself, for to seem to seek and enjoy influence is, in large part, to lose it.

8

Kinship and Territorial Groups

Kinship

MAI The notion of *mai* is crucial to an understanding of Semai social organization. Literally, *mai* means simply "they," but the Semai often use the word in the sense of "they-as-opposed-to-us." Thus, the phrase "he's *mai*" can mean "he's a stranger," "he's from another *gu*," or, in the commonest usage, "he isn't a consanguineal[1] kinsman of mine."

Like most people all over the world, the Semai make the distinction between "we" and *mai* the basis of a value judgment. Implicit in their often repeated claim that "we never get angry" is the assertion "*mai* get angry." The Semai say that one can never rely on *mai* to help one out or even to refrain from doing one harm. When a man shrugs and says, "It's the affair of *mai*," he means that he has no rights or duties in the affair under discussion. The Semai do not trust *mai* but say, sometimes rather ruefully, "We're all very, very suspicious of *mai*." In short, *mai* are unpredictable and possibly dangerous people, best left alone.

Even if a Semai has a cordial relationship with a person who is *mai* to him, he tends to express it in terms of consanguineal ties. For instance, when people became comfortable with us, they began to use kinship terms to address us. Another example is the metaphor given in Chapter 1 about the *gu:* "We have the same great-grandparents of great-grandparents." People add, however, that this seemingly consanguineal tie is really a fiction, "just a tale of the old people." That is, some of the people in one's *gu* are really *mai*, with whose affairs one cannot be much concerned. Similarly, two east Semai who like each other may set up a *kakasih* or "friendship" relationship with each other. The two parties, who are always of the same sex, agree to help each other "like siblings," that is, like close consanguineal kinsmen. They hope that their children will marry each other so that their grandchildren will not be *mai* to each other. Such friendships are voluntary, however, and either party may break off the relationship at any time, for any reason.

---

[1] Consanguineal—descended from the same ancestor(s).

71

CONSANGUINEAL KINSHIP Thus, the only relationships in which a Semai can feel really secure are those between consanguineal kinsmen. This is not to say that even such kinship is sufficient in and of itself to create a close emotional tie. A person has to cultivate the affection of his kinsmen. He has the option of building ties of mutual aid and cordiality or, alternatively, of ignoring the relationship. If the consanguineal bond is not cultivated, he expects and receives no more from a kinsman than from a covillager or casual acquaintance.

The east Semai will go to considerable lengths to discover a consanguineal tie with a Semai stranger, for example, a west Semai visitor. However tenuous the relationship, people will cling to it because it transforms the visitor from a potentially dangerous *mai* person to a more trustworthy kinsman. People seemed to be yet more comfortable with my wife and myself after they began to address us in kinship terms.

The west Semai set more rigid limits to consanguineal ties. Only people in a person's *jeg* are his consanguineal kinsmen. The *jeg* is the set of all the descendants of one's great-grandparents, not including the great-grandparents themselves. The Semai say that a person is fortunate if each of his grandparents came from a different settlement. He is fortunate because if for any reason he leaves his settlement he can go to live with his consanguineal kinsmen instead of with the always untrustworthy *mai*. Although sometimes people use consanguineal kinship terminology for referring to people outside their *jeg*, the relationship is really "just a tale of the old people."

The importance of age in Semai society, discussed in the section on elders in the previous chapter, finds expression in the fact that most of the distinctions made in Semai kinship terminology depend on relative age and generation. A Semai refers to all his consanguineal kinsmen in his own generation as *tɔne'* if they are older than he is, *mɔnang* if they are younger. The children of *tɔne'* he refers to by the same term he uses for his own children,[2] and he similarly classes the children of *mɔnang* with his own grandchildren. All consanguineal kinsmen in his grandchildren's generation are referred to by the same term as his own grandchildren, and all consanguineal kinsmen in his grandparent's generation are referred to as "grandmother," "grandfather," or "grandparent." There are special words for mother, father, parent's male *tɔne'*, parent's female *tɔne'*, parent's male *mɔnang*, and parent's female *mɔnang*.

This terminology both reflects and enhances the importance of relative age and generation in defining proper respect patterns within a Semai community. A *tɔne'* may be male or female, sibling or cousin. What is important about a *tɔne'*, however, is that he is (1) in one's own generation so that one can be at ease with him and (2) older than oneself so that one should respect his opinions, for example, by listening to ("hearing") them. A person in an older generation than one's one rates more respect than a *tɔne'*, for example, he should be addressed as "you" (*jɔən*, west Semai) or "you two" (*jɔɔn*, east Semai). Reciprocally, he calls one "thou" and need not pay much attention to one's opinions. Although the Semai state no specific rule, in general the amount of deference a younger party owes an older one is proportionate to the age and generational gap between them.

---

[2] Some west Semai use a Malay phrase for the children of *tɔne'*.

One advantage of classifying cousins and siblings together under the same set of terms[3] is that a Semai can extend these terms to any person with whom he thinks he has some consanguineal tie, even though he is not sure just how they are related. On the one hand, then, a Semai can choose from among a wide range of possible consanguineal ties those which he wishes to emphasize. On the other hand, outside his own family he is not constrained to accept the duties of any particular kinship tie unless he wants to do so.

MARRIAGE   Under this system marriage becomes a focus of anxiety. An east Semai should not marry any consanguineal kinsman, and a west Semai should not marry anyone descended from one of his grandparents. Most marriages must therefore be with *mai,* that is, with precisely the least trustworthy people around. In the east, where settlements are relatively small, there are often no unwed *mai* of the right age and sex to marry. Even in the west, where settlements are larger, almost 70 percent of the marriages involve people from different settlements. In short, not only is a spouse usually *mai* in terms of consanguineal kinship, he or she is doubly *mai* in that he or she is likely to come from a different settlement.

The anxiety this situation engenders is reflected in the pattern of residence after marriage. Typically, the newlyweds spend a week or two with the wife's family, then a month or so with the husband's family. They may then return to the wife's settlement for a year or two, and so on at gradually increasing intervals, until they finally settle down once and for all. Even while this shuttling is going on, the couple periodically separate, each person going on week- or month-long visits to his or her consanguineal kinsmen.

There is no explicit rule constraining people to behave this way. The reasons the Semai give for the shuttling and extended visiting are "homesickness" (*rəniag*) and mistrust of *mai.* A newlywed cut off from consanguineal kinsmen and covillagers feels cut off from meaningful human contacts. For example, one newly married east Semai man living in his wife's house with thirty of her relatives asked me to write a letter begging his elder brother to visit him. "I can't stand it here," he said, "all alone by myself."

Obviously, this sort of situation puts a great strain on a marriage. The east and west Semai have developed two different solutions to this problem: in the east, strictly defining relations between in-laws, and in the west, a particular sort of wedding ceremony.

The east Semai have no wedding ceremonies. As a result, it is sometimes hard to tell whether a couple are "married" or just having an affair. Temporary separations are equally hard to differentiate from divorce. Since there are no Semai words for "marriage" or "divorce," people have to talk about these topics in Malay. Sometimes the Semai themselves seem unsure about whether a certain person is married or not. For example, one girl told us on our arrival that she was married to a man who had been away for about a year. About three months later she had still not heard from him and was saying, "I *think* I'm not married any more." In another case, a man who had slept with a certain girl only once sometimes referred to the episode as a "marriage" but at other times said it was "just playing around." The girl in question, who had decided that she did not like him, said that she had slept

---

[3] Anthropologists call this "Hawaiian" or "generational" cousin terminology.

with him but had never been married to him. This conceptual haziness makes it easy to slip into or out of marriage. Consequently, there are few east Semai adults who do not report that they have been "married" and "divorced" more than once, occasionally as many as eight or nine times. If two people eat together, sleep in the same room, cooperate in economic activities, and call each other "husband" and "wife," then other people in their settlement will say that they are married. There are, of course, many long lasting, stable marriages of this kind. On the whole, the longer two people have been married, the more likely they are to stay married. The main exception is when a husband takes another wife, in which case his first wife is likely to leave him. Since wives are not supposed to take more than one husband (very rarely, one does), taking a new man almost automatically means losing the old one.

East Semai marriage does not constrain a person's sexual activities very tightly. Transitory premarital and extramarital affairs are taken lightly, especially if one's spouse is sick, away visiting, or under some sort of ritual restriction like the one that prohibits a woman from having sexual intercourse for two years after bearing a child. People say of such affairs, "It's all right, it's just a loan." To object would be *kareid,* "selfish," or "stingy" and, more seriously, it might be conducive to *punan.* As *punan* it is, of course, grounds for divorce. Illegitimacy under these circumstances is amusing, but not the serious problem it is some kin-based societies.

The east Semai deal with the problem of how to tolerate associating with a person's spouse's family by explicitly defining "proper" behavior in such relationships. To all one's in-laws who are older than one's spouse and of the opposite sex to oneself, one behaves with great deference, which is reciprocated. East Semai in such relationships should not address each other, eat together, look directly at each other, speak each other's names, sit or walk close together, sleep in the same room, or be alone together. Theoretically, a breach of these rules, especially in the case of a man and his mother-in-law, is equivalent to incest and will bring disaster to all involved. In fact, however, the Semai often bend the rules a little, especially if the age difference between the two parties is not too great.

To all one's in-laws who are older than one's spouse and of the same sex as oneself one shows some deference, which is reciprocated. An east Semai may talk, eat, and work with such kinsmen. He may not talk about sex or argue with them, however, nor will he engage in horseplay with them. The two parties address each other with the formal pronoun "you-two" instead of the more usual "thou." The sort of deference they deserve is reflected in the kinship terminology. The word for mother-in-law is a modification of the word for grandmother, and the words for spouse's elder siblings come from the words for parent's elder siblings.

As time goes on and the marriage endures, people came to know and like each other. Consequently, the great respect they are required to show each other becomes a little chafing. They then have the option of moderating the deference they show each other and even if they have become very fond of each other, of changing the kinship terminology they use. For example, a man who has become friendly with his mother-in-law may call her "grandmother" and treat her with the lesser deference due one's grandmother. The east Semai say that it is admirable for a man to call his mother-in-law "mother," but stress that most people would be too embarrassed to do so, probably because the tensions are usually too great. Similarly, a woman who finds a man attractive but is his wife's elder sister may apt to be called "wife's younger sister," *mənai.*

The relations between a spouse's younger sibling and an elder sibling's spouse are supposed to be free and easy. The two parties refer to each other as *mənai,* a word derived from the word *mai. Mənai* are, as it were, modified *mai,* modified in the sense that the dangerous aggressiveness attributed to *mai* here finds its outlet in socially approved, harmless joking and horseplay. The jokes typically involve sex or aggression, for example, "Admit you copulate with chickens!" or "Don't sleep here, sleep in the river!" The horseplay involves actions like pretending to pull down a *mənai's* sarong at a dance or to ram a corncob up a *mənai's* vagina. Opposite-sexed *mənai* have free sexual access to each other whether or not they are married.

Besides providing a relief for the tensions of living with in-laws, the *mənai* relationship serves as a kind of life insurance. Since a man has probably already had sexual relations with his elder brother's wife, he is more likely to marry her and look after her if his elder brother dies before him. Conversely, a widower may get aid and comfort from his wife's younger sister. The Semai regard such secondary marriages as praiseworthy, although no pressure is put on the people involved to marry.

The west Semai have evolved a completely different solution to the problem of living with in-laws. There, one defers to all one's in-laws including *mənai.* The older they are, the more one defers to them, but the deference consists at most in not quarreling, talking about sex, or engaging in horseplay with them. Again, people think that calling a parent-in-law "parent" is a good thing, and there are a few people who are not "embarrassed" to do so.

The west Semai solution to the tensions of marriage involves the wedding ceremony which, with some modifications, is based on Malay weddings. The bride and groom sit together on a mat on one side of the room. An elder of the village stands behind them and asks a public blessing, the couple exchange cigarettes, and they are legally married. This type of ceremony is found even among some east Semai.

The unique part of the west Semai ceremony is the system of "payments" (*bəlanja'*) and wedding lectures. The groom's kinsmen should give the equivalent of about 21 U.S. dollars to the bride's kinsmen, with the bride getting about half the payment. Furthermore, each party pays about $1.08 to the headman of the settlement in which the wedding occurs. The fact that payments less than the amount set by custom are acceptable shows that the payment is essentially symbolic, although the groom's party is "embarrassed" if they cannot collect the full amount from the groom's consanguineal kinsmen. The money is spread out on cloth after the public blessing, so that everyone present can see that it has been paid. The headman takes his share as a sign that he will take an interest in the continuing stability of the marriage. The bride's mother's younger brother accepts part of the remaining money, rejecting the rest as a sign that although the bride's consanguineal kinsmen are giving up part of their interest in her welfare they are not giving it up entirely.

Then, for about an hour, the elders one by one lecture the audience. They explain that if the groom or his consanguineal kinsmen maltreat or embarrass the bride they will lose their rights to the return of the money that they have paid. They tell the bride and her consanguineal kinsmen that the money is not for their profit, to make them rich. If they meddle in the marriage they will lose it. The bride is not to spend her share on clothes or movies, but rather to save it for emergencies or paying fines in the event she behaves badly toward her husband. She should not listen to gossip about her husband. Even if she has reason to think he is flirting with another woman, she should take no action until the third or fourth time and then she should not complain to her consanguineal kinsmen but to the groom's mother's younger brother. She will naturally be afraid, the elders say, living in a strange settlement, but she should remember that this evening she was married and ought to stay with her husband, be he rich or be he poor. There is a good deal more lecturing in this vein, often until the bride is in tears. The elders then turn their attention to the groom and give him a similar lecture.

There are two important things to recognize about this ceremony. First, both parties come at least symbolically to have some pecuniary interest in keeping the marriage going. Second, the bride and groom are forcefully told that they are not to rely on their own consanguineal kinsmen in case of a marital spat. The angry wife is told not to go home to mother. She must rely on *mai,* on her husband's consanguineal kinsmen, as he must rely on hers. The kinsmen, in turn, have obligated themselves to care for *mai,* their kinsman's spouse. Should a newlywed complain to her own people first, they are likely to be unsympathetic, since they have to pay the fine involved. In short, where the east Semai keep in-laws at a distance or joke with them, the west Semai throw the newlyweds into their in-law's arms.

It is worth noting that west Semai marriages seem to be more stable than those of the east Semai. It looks as though their system works better. Extramarital and premarital affairs are frowned upon. If a west Semai man refused to marry a girl he has impregnated, however, she can always give her child to her consanguineal kinsmen, who will be eager to adopt it. The result is that legitimacy is not of much importance.

In summary, with the exception of the obligations imposed by the west Semai wedding ceremony, kinship is not for the Semai the cage of rules that it is for some peoples. Rather, kinship provides a potential set of relationships which the individual can exploit or not, as he wishes. He has great freedom about which kin ties he wants to emphasize, whom he wants to marry, how friendly he wants to be with his in-laws.

Territorial Groups

HOUSEHOLD AND HOMESTEAD   The people who live together in a Semai house are usually related to one another. The main relationships that lead the Semai to live together are those of the nuclear family, that is, parents live with their children, siblings live together. Kinship ties between adult but not aged men seem to be of prime importance in determining who lives with whom. The typical focus of a coresidential group is a set of brothers or brothers-in-law, although it may be a father and his son(s) or a pair of cousins. Other people join the group by virtue of their relationship, direct or indirect, to these central figures. The importance of these men seems to rest on the fact that they do the bulk of the work of housebuilding and, therefore, have primary responsibility for deciding whether or not to live together.

The dominant living arrangement in the west is a cluster of small houses that form a homestead. In the east these same kinsmen are likely to live together in the same house, although homesteads do occur. Since the make up and activities of east Semai households and west Semai homesteads are very similar, both may be classed as "house groups" for purposes of discussion. The houses themselves are described in Chapter 1.

East Semai houses hold an average of fourteen people, but may include as many as fifty-four. West Semai houses hold an average of about five people and do not include more than twenty-four. About a quarter of the eastern settlements consist of a single house, constituting a "longhouse community." In the west there are few or no longhouse communities, and over half the houses contain only a single nuclear family.

Ethnologists think that all Semai once lived in multifamily longhouses, as the more isolated groups still do. Within a longhouse each nuclear family has its own sleeping compartment, with widowed adults and unmarried adolescents usually sleeping in the central area. The "ownership" of sleeping compartments is rather like the "ownership" of fields discussed in Chapter 4. That is, a nuclear family has exclusive rights over its compartment as long as the members are actively using it. If they go away on a prolonged visit, however, as Semai often do, then another nuclear family may move in, and pre-empt the compartment. On their return the original "owners" have to work out new sleeping arrangements, perhaps in another house. To some extent this principle seems to apply to nuclear family houses as well. The east Semai say that deserted houses are likely to attract "evil spirits" (*nyani'*), much as deserted houses in America are sometimes said to be "haunted." The Semai would therefore be leery of moving into an abandoned house and usually prefer to burn it down. My wife and I, however, did move into "deserted" houses in each of the two settlements we lived in, only to have the original owners return. In neither case did anyone but us make a fuss. In fact, our relationship with the former owners was remarkably warm, perhaps because the Semai expect that two people who have slept in the same place will be bound by a sort of sympathetic tie.

Inside the longhouse the nuclear families of two or three siblings will often cook over a common hearth. Usually the women prepare food separately for their families. If two women who share a hearth both want to cook at the same time, however, either both will prepare a common meal or one will go to cook over another hearth.

At adolescence a person is expected to move out of his or her parents' sleeping compartment. If there is a vacant compartment in the house, two adolescent boys or two adolescent girls may sleep there. Should a new nuclear family move into the house, however, the adolescents must give up their compartment to the newcomers and sleep in the central area or move out of the house. The result is that adolescents, especially boys, often have to move from house to house. They decide which household they want to join on the basis of kinship and friendship. Normally, an adolescent boy prefers to move in with his married brother or sister, but boys moved even into our tiny house on two occasions for prolonged stays.

This adolescent pattern illustrates the point, made earlier in this chapter, that most kinship ties have to be cultivated to be significant in Semai society. The people in a longhouse are almost always kinsmen. Kinship by itself, however, does not bring adult Semai to live together. There must also be a bond of mutual liking and respect, especially between the adult men of a household. Since there is no formal leadership and no set way of resolving quarrels in a longhouse, any dispute is likely to fracture the bond of friendship, with the result that one party will move out and set up housekeeping elsewhere. Moving out poses few problems, since one man working hard can build in a week or two a house big enough to accommodate two or three nuclear families.

The membership of a longhouse is thus constantly in flux. Adolescent boys move in and out. Quarrelers withdraw, taking their sympathizers with them. People get divorced and move out, usually accompanied by their consanguineal kinsmen. A person who was one of the focal figures in one longhouse eventually becomes an aged dependent in another. The east Semai custom of building new houses every year or so often leads to a complete reshuffling of house groups. Only rarely does a longhouse keep the same membership for many years.

Contact with non-Semai seems to break down the longhouse arrangement into homesteads of nuclear family houses. I cannot document this change for either of the groups with which we lived. However, census records show that a number of southeast Semai settlements went from the longhouse pattern to the homestead pattern in half a dozen years after the Malayan government opened up the area for settlement by Malays and Chinese. Three factors may underlie the shift from the east Semai longhouse to the west Semai homestead. First, as mentioned in Chapter 3, the longhouse serves as a refuge against wild animals that have become relatively rare in the west. Second, west Semai living arrangements may in part be modeled on those of the Malays, who usually live in homesteads rather than in multifamily houses. Finally, the west Semai often work for wages and usually buy many of their household needs. A person can support his family by his individual efforts. In the east, as noted in Chapter 5, an individual depends more on other people to meet the needs of himself and his family. In brief, where the nuclear family is the basic unit of production and consumption, nuclear family households are the rule; whereas where the unit of production and consumption is larger, households are larger.

Inasmuch as the homestead seems to be a broken-up longhouse, it is not surprising that the kinship structure is like that of a longhouse. A typical household in a homestead includes a nuclear family. It may also include people who cannot support themselves, for example, a widowed parent, or an unmarried orphan sibling. People usually sleep in the same room and cook over a single hearth.

Although rights to fields and crops are vested in the nuclear family, members of an east or west Semai house group usually clear mutually adjacent fields. The house group helps in tasks a married couple cannot perform alone, notably, felling large trees and planting major crops. Cohouseholders usually cooperate to build their own house, the women doing the roofing, and the men doing the rest. The women of a house group typically go together to collect field produce or to fish. After meeting the needs of his wife and children, a Semai will offer surplus food to other members of the house group. Members of a house group also often ask for and get food in small quantities from each other.

Although the parents take the main responsibility for rearing children, the house group also plays a part. The west Semai make this sharing of responsibility explicit. A parent has to consult with all the adults in his house group before he makes any important decision about the child's welfare, for example, whether or not to send a child to the hospital. Two proverbs explain the proper behavior of the people involved. The father should say, "My wife is my wife; my child, the child of others." The child's grandparents and parent's elder siblings should say, "My child is my child; my grandchild, the grandchild of others." (A person's older siblings call his child their "grandchild.")

West Semai householders observe certain rice rituals when the household's fields are being harvested. The harvest in, they feast their fellow homesteaders and the families of covillagers in their *jeg*. Before eating, one of the adult men of the household asks a blessing from the guests and sprinkles them with water in which certain magical plants have been steeped. The rituals during the harvest are based on Malay rituals, and the entire custom may be a borrowing from the Malays.

In summary, the familiar Semai pattern obtains here. Groups are unstable, and there is no position available that would allow one person to constrain the behavior of others.

BAND The Semai band is a group of people who see each other often. It has a definable territory called a "land" (*tei'*) and takes its name from a prominent geographical feature of that territory, usually a small stream. Each band has a nominal headman and sometimes an assistant headman. Each band is autonomous with respect to any other band.

A Semai settlement is a residential unit composed of houses less than fifteen minutes' walk from each other and normally separated from other settlements by about an hour's walk. Usually, all the members of a band live in a single settlement, but two settlement bands are not uncommon, and there are even a few bands comprising three or more settlements.

East Semai bands average 45 people and rarely range over 100. West Semai bands average 70 people and rarely over 200. For a variety of reasons band size seems to have been increasing in the last fifty years. First, government pressure and occasional dispossession of Semai bands in the west sometimes forces two bands to amalgamate. Second, with the outlawing of the slave trade, large Semai bands are no longer a tempting target for Malay slavers. Third, rice and the American crops are more productive than the traditional crops and so permit denser concentrations of population.

Except for longhouse communities, Semai settlements tend to sprawl so that each house can be in or near its field. In the hilly highlands, people prefer to build houses in cleared areas on hill tops. In the west, villages sometimes consist of permanent houses built close together, surrounded by a sprawl of temporary field houses (see Chapter 4).

Like the other social units of the Semai, the band is unstable, especially in the east. The two reasons most often given for moving out of a band are quarrels and "homesickness" (rəniag), but a person may leave a band for the same reasons he would leave a house group. Other reasons for changing band affiliation include preferring another headman, being jilted, being unable to find a spouse, and finding one's surroundings intolerable because one's beloved child has died there.

People typically leave a band between the time of harvest and clearing new fields, the time the band itself is likely to move to a different part of its territory. At this time people who have postponed leaving because of the difficulties of moving are likely to break away. The break-away groups, usually households, may stay in the band's territory as settlements within the band, or they may move into the territory of another band.

The bond between a band and its "land" is less a matter of ownership than of sentiment. This is where one's parents and children are buried, or where one was born, the place for which one feels the bittersweet yearning the Semai call rəniag. The land is home, not a commodity to be owned. No one has exclusive rights over the land. Anyone, whether a band member or not, can clear a field on it. The failure to recognize that non-Semai think of land as something to be bought and sold, a concept totally alien to the Semai, has been a fertile source of misunderstanding and quarrels between the Semai and their non-Semai neighbors. Semai headmen sometimes will accept small sums of money for the land and then, when the buyer asserts exclusive rights over it, they feel cheated and become profoundly bitter. One of the constant fears of the Semai is that, by processes they do not clearly understand, *mai* are going to take away Semai land.

Gu   The *gu,* described in Chapter 1, was once merely the product of the geographic environment, without much social significance. To be sure, one headman in a *gu* might by sheer force of personality have been able to influence some other headmen, but there was no formal leadership. When the Communist rebels took to the highlands in 1952–1953, however, the Semai were faced with a problem unique in their history. For the first time, armed bands of *mai* (the Communists and the government forces) were roving through Semai territory. The terrified Semai felt driven to devise some solution that would keep them from being caught in the middle.

The Communist terrorists inadvertently provided the key to the solution of the problem. They began using the *gu* as the basis for so-called "*ASAL* clubs,"[4] whose members were to provide intelligence and logistic support for the insurgents. In 1953 some influential Temiar headmen within one *gu* met and devised a six-point program that in true Senoi manner substituted duplicity for open confrontation with *mai.* The Semai quickly adopted the program. The six points of the program were the following: (1) Bands upstream and thus near the Communists were to aver that they supported the Communists. (2) Bands down river in contact with

---

[4] *ASAL* is Malay for "origin." The Malayan aborigines are officially called Orang Asali or Orang Aseli, "People of Ancient Origin."

the government forces were to "support" the government. (3) The "pro-Communist" and "pro-government" bands were to keep each other informed of the plans of *mai*. (4) The majority of the people, who were between these two groups, were to play dumb, which the Semai do superbly. "We're just stupid dirty aborigines," they were to say. "We live and die in the jungle like animals. We know nothing." These midstream people were to provide food and shelter on demand to *mai*. They were not to supply guides and bearers except for a good cash consideration. They were not to ask the troops' plans or destinations. (5) No information was to be given *mai* that might endanger any Semai or lead to a battle for which the Semai might be blamed. (6) In the event of a Communist victory, the "pro-Communist" bands were to cover up for all the bands downstream from them, claiming that all had been pro-Communist. Conversely, if the government won, the "pro-government" bands were to cover for the bands upstream.

This innovation spread to all the Semai affected by the conflict. In fact, it is still in operation to some extent, notably in the east. Although the Malayan government is working hard to promote Semai welfare, the Semai remain suspicious that the government programs may be elaborate ruses to deprive the Semai of their land. The down-river groups often cooperate, partly to cover for the up-river groups. Many of the up-river groups maintain a pose of impenetrable stupidity which is only now yielding to the efforts of the dedicated officials of the Department of Aborigines of the Malayan government.

In short, the *gu* has been transformed from a unit with no political function into an organization whose sole aim is to coordinate efforts to baffle and frustrate the outsiders who are trying to penetrate and change Semai society. Perhaps it is significant that the only stimulus sufficient to make the Semai give up a little of their individual and band autonomy is the incursion of *mai*. Even in this case, however, the surrender of autonomy is voluntary and unenforceable, based on shared mistrust of *mai*.

9

Disease, Death, and Medicine

Thinking about Disease

BASIC CONCEPTS   The Semai think of a person as made up of a set of six interlocking things or processes. The two most important components of this complex are *ruai* or "soul" and *kəloog* or "spirit." The *səngii'* or "thought" is localized in the heart and expressed in the *ləhəm* or "breath." The other two elements of a person are his *səkoo'* or "aura," which can be seen as the flush of good health in the face of a robust person, and the *nadi* or "arterial pulse," which is primarily located where it is most strongly felt, in the left breast.

The Semai language is not rich in words that describe the relationships between concepts. To get around this difficulty, the Semai rely heavily on metaphor. The relationships among this set of things with which you are unfamiliar, a Semai says in effect, are the same as the relationships among *that* set of things, which you already understand. This use of metaphors that refer to relationships the listener has personally experienced gives Semai science a vividness and immediacy that Euro-American science often lacks. For example, Daylight, a sensitive and intellectual west Semai man, says that to grasp the relationships between the six components of a person one can think of a person as a car. *Ruai* would be the battery, *kəloog* the driver, "thought" the running of the engine, "breath" the gas, "aura" the paint, and "arterial pulse" the speedometer.

The metaphor is brilliant, even for a Semai, and I feel bad about subjecting Daylight's succinct and vivid description to a relatively long-winded and pedestrian exposition. *Ruai* is the spark that keeps a person going, without which he "runs down." *Kəloog* is the process, something like "will," whereby he governs his activities. "Thought" is like the stream of consciousness. Breathing supplies him with fuel for his actions. His "aura" is a "glow of health" that fades when he becomes old or sick. Finally, the arterial pulse is used even by Euro-American physicians to gauge how well a person is "running." In the discussion of disease, *ruai* and *kəloog* play the most significant role.

Ruai is located just behind the center of the forehead. The Semai describe it

82

in three ways. First, it is a human being, the image of the body it inhibits, about three-quarters of an inch tall. On occasion it assumes the form of an animal. Second, it is a little bird. Third, it is a timid child. At night *ruai* leave the body and travel around. While traveling they meet other *ruai* and their experiences are manifested in dreams of people or animals, especially birds. Sometimes in its travels a *ruai* falls under the sway of an "evil spirit" or *nyani'*. Sometimes *ruai* is frightened away by a startling event. Loss of *ruai* is especially common in children because their *ruai* and hearts are weak. Almost all Semai adults report having suffered *ruai* loss as children. The observable symptoms of *ruai* loss are listlessness, diarrhea, weeping, and fever. These symptoms are especially pronounced if the *ruai* has fallen into the power of *nyani'*.

Unlike *ruai*, *kəloog* is formless. It also may leave the body, but its absence is more serious. If it is gone more than a week or two, the patient dies. During *ruai* loss, *kəloog* may also depart, but it remains nearer the body than *ruai* does.

These concepts are not to be dismissed as superstitions. They serve as ways in which thoughtful men organize their experience of life, death, and dream. Any observer can see that when a man dies, his "aura," "breath," and "arterial pulse" go away. To say that his *kəloog* has gone is as sensible as to say that his "life" has gone. In this sense *kəloog*, in fact, might be translated as "life," but the term also refers to the feeling any human being has of being able to decide to do something. In this sense *kəloog* is translatable as "will" or "consciousness." The point is that *kəloog* refers to experiences which all people have. The Semai conceptualization of these experiences divides them up in a different way from, say, the American conceptualization. The notion of *kəloog* is not mystical, just different.

Similarly, unlike most Euro-Americans, the Semai take some types of dreams to be valid experiences.[1] There are dreams, called *pipuui*, that the Semai dismiss. These are nightmares of falling, dreams in which the dreamer obtains something he wants like a winning lottery number, or the like. Valid dreams (*mənakei'*), however, are to be taken seriously. Such dreams, says a wise west Semai man, are the basis of religion. The notion of *ruai* serves to resolve a problem posed by dreaming. On the one hand, the dreamer himself is unconscious, which is to say that his *kəloog* is gone, although not so far that it cannot return in a moment if he is awakened. The dreamer's body is inert. On the other hand, he has experiences of far places, of flying, or of other people. If these experiences are valid, then there must be some part of the dreamer which has left his inert body and is having the experiences. This traveling being is what the Semai call *ruai*. It is birdlike in being able to fly over vast distances. It is manlike in that it has the identity of the dreamer. It is childlike in that it is easily frightened. The symptoms of *ruai* loss are after all perfectly visible and completely explicable in terms of a timid *ruai*.

To try to cram such useful Semai concepts as *ruai* and *kəloog* into one of the English categories "spiritual" or "material" would be to distort them. The question of whether *ruai* is a thing, a spirit, or a process does not arise in Semai ideology.

NYANI' The verb *nyi'* or *nya'nyi'* means, roughly, to feel pain. The noun *nya'ni'* formed from this verb therefore means something like "pain" or "painful

---

[1] Recently, the Euro-American view of dreams seems to be coming closer to that of the Semai, under the joint influence of psychoanalysis and the "mind-expanding" drugs.

bodily condition." There are conditions like nearsightedness, stammering, and certain skin diseases which are not classified as *nya'ni'* because they do not cause pain. Most of the other conditions which a Euro-American doctor would call "disease" the Semai call *nya'ni'*.

The relationship between the words *nya'ni'* and *nyani'* is comprehensible by an analogy with two other words that are structurally related in the same way. *Cha'na'* is "food," a "meal," or "eating." *Chana'* is cooked rice. A Semai may have a meal without eating cooked rice, but he will say that he has not really eaten, because a meal without cooked rice does not make him feel "full" (*bahei'*). Rice is thus a central part of the category "meal" so that the word for "cooked rice" derives from the word for meal. (All Senoi-speakers who have grown rice for a long time call cooked rice *chana'*; but the east Semai and others who have been newly introduced to rice call it by the Malay word *nasi*.) Similarly the concept of *nyani'* is the central part of the category *nya'ni'*, and the word *nyani'* seems to be derived from the word for a painful disease.

As there are meals without cooked rice, so there are *nya'ni'* without *nyani'*. The Semai attribute insect stings, cuts, bruises, and burns to physical causes. Most of the time, however, there is no visible agent that produces disease. One way of translating *nyani'* is "invisible agent of disease."

But *nyani'* are not always invisible. *Ruai* can see *nyani'*, as attested by dreams. The Semai sometimes speak of *nyani'* as if the concept was deduced from experience. For example, contagion is an argument for the existence of *nyani'*. People with a sickness, the Semai say, carry the *nyani'* that causes the sickness around with them, with the result that if one person in a house falls sick of a certain *nyani'*, then the *nyani'* will attack other people in the same house. In this sense, the concept of *nyani'* is no more supernatural than the Euro-American concept of "disease." But the Semai also talk of having seen the red eyes of *nyani'* gleaming in the dark, of having heard them gibber, squeak, and murmur as they rustle through a thatched roof. Some *nyani'* are quite visible, like the nocturnal house cricket that the Semai burn to death whenever they catch it. Other *nyani'* have no shape or form at all outside of dreams. Whenever a Semai talks of *nyani'* it is as hard to tell whether the speaker is talking about a given entity or about a class of entities as it is to tell whether the English word "tuberculosis" refers to a single entity or to a class of entities. The Semai do not seem to worry about whether the concept *nyani'* refers to something singular or plural, material or spiritual, personal or impersonal. Unlike English, the Semai language does not force people to make such distinctions.

Some *nyani'*, like "tree *nyani'* " and "water *nyani'*," have specific habitats. Most of the *nyani'* that underlie specific human ailments, however, seem to drop from human ken when not actively molesting people. People have to pause and think for a while before they can decide where such *nyani'* live. Even after some thought, they can only say that *nyani'* live somewhere "out there in the hills." Similarly, different people give different accounts of how *nyani'* operate. For example, the *nyani' panali'* which causes hepatitis and tuberculosis, usually attacks only when someone has mixed together categories of food that should be eaten separately (see Chapter 3). Sometimes, however, people talk as if the mixing of foods can mechanically bring about the disease without the active intervention of *nyani'*. Sometimes *nyani'* are said to enter the victim's body and "eat" it from within. Sometimes they are said to capture the victim's *ruai*. The only thing that all Semai always agree on is that *nyani'* cause diseases not attributable to observable agents.

In short, to call *nyani'* "evil spirits" is to distort the Semai concept, which is both more abstract and more concrete than the word "spirit" conveys. Like *ruai* and *kɔloog*, the term *nyani'* eludes any neat translation into English.

HALAA' Although to the Semai way of thinking, dreams prove that any-one's *ruai* may come across *nyani'*, only people who are *halaa'* can send *ruai* to seek out the *nyani'* that make a certain person sick. A man becomes *halaa'* by having a dream in which he is given a melody. The dream figure which supplies the melody is usually a *ruai*, but also is often a *kɔloog* belonging to an animal or sometimes to a person or *nyani'*. Very few animals of any given species have *ruai* or *kɔloog*. Of all animals tigers have probably the highest proportion of individuals with *ruai* or *kɔloog*. Winds and rivers, although most people say they have no *ruai* or *kɔloog*, sometimes give melodies in dreams "because the wind is the airplane of *nyani'* and the river their steamboat." The donor of the melody then becomes the *gunig* of the dreamer. When, during the "sings" described later in this chapter, the dreamer sings the melody, the *ruai* or *kɔloog* of his *gunig* will come to him. He can then ask it what *nyani'* are causing a given affliction and, speaking through or to him, it will tell him. Similarly, he can send it off to save a captured *ruai*.

There is no question that the Semai actually do get melodies in dreams. For example, one east Semai man fell deeply in love with a girl upstream who wanted no part of him. For weeks he mooned in misery. Finally, he dreamed that she gave him a melody. His depression lifted at once, for the melody proved that his dream was not merely *pipuui*. "Another man has her body," he says, grinning, "but I have her *ruai*."

There are varying degrees of *halaa'*.[2] Women are very rarely more than just a little *halaa'*, but a really *halaa'* woman is more successful than most male *halaa'* in the diagnosis and cure of diseases. There are two ways to tell how *halaa'* someone is. The first is to find how many *gunig* he has. The more *gunig*, the more *halaa'*. The second and more reliable test is how successful he is in his endeavors, mainly, curing people. Even animals which are continually successful, like dogs which almost always put up game, are *halaa'* in this sense.

By this second way of reckoning, *halaa'* powers fluctuate. The Semai assess how *halaa'* a person is by the number of people who have recovered after he has treated them. A *halaa'* who has had great success becomes well known, and even Malays and Chinese may seek him out for his curative powers. On the other hand, if he loses a patient, he is clearly less *halaa'* than he was. The west Semai say he has become *jah*, which they explain metaphorically as: "He has lost his salt." The rela-tives of the deceased patient then should ritually bathe the *halaa'* in water made fragrant by magical herbs so that he will again become attractive to his *gunig*. As a man gets older, he becomes less and less able to perform the strenuous singing and dancing required of a *halaa'* so that he may in effect retire.

The relationship between a *halaa'* and his *gunig* is very close, "like that of a

---

[2] Properly, *halaa'* is a verb or adjective; *mai halaa'* are people who possess the quality; the quality itself is *hanalaa'*.

father with his children." He does not eat the meat of animals that belong to the same species as his *gunig*. If the gunig is Malay, the *halaa'* follows Malay food taboos. In the northern hilly parts of the west Semai territory a *halaa'* can transfer his *gunig* to another man, provided that the *gunig* "likes the other man's body." *Gunig* are as erratic as people about whom they are attracted to. Most Semai, however, say that the bond between a *gunig* and its "father" is too strong to be broken. When a *halaa'* dies, his *gunig* seek a new "father," sometimes en masse. Very often they appear in the dreams of a brother or son of the dead *halaa'* and ask him to take them on by holding a special sort of "sing."

Like all *ruai,* and indeed like the Semai themselves, the *ruai* of the *gunig* are timid. They will appear only in the dark. A sudden sound or sneeze will frighten them away. The presence of a pair of anthropologists almost always made these *ruai* very nervous. People had to explain that we were "just like Semai," living and eating like Semai. Even so, the ever suspicious *ruai* would ask, for example, "If they're so friendly, why are they always writing in those little books?" If the *ruai gunig* are frightened away, then their "father" must hold a special "sing" of the sort described below in order to placate them.

Treatment

HOME REMEDIES   When a Semai feels under the weather, he doses himself with home remedies that he has used before with apparent success. Almost everyone has a few personal remedies, usually sour or bitter decoctions made of plant juices. He also thinks back to see whether he can remember eating anything that might have brought on his (or his child's) discomfort. For example, the parents of a child whose eyes are red from continuous weeping may recall that a few weeks earlier they ate a red-eyed civet cat. The red eyes of the civet, they might conclude, as one couple did, are responsible for the child's condition. Henceforward, they will be careful about eating civet. If eating a certain food is followed two or three times by sickness, the patient (or parent) stops eating the food. For this reason many Semai say that they do not "understand" (are allergic to eating) certain foods.

This sort of after the fact reasoning is fallacious from the viewpoint of Euro-American science. The east Semai belief that eating sweets predisposes one to malaria, for example, is almost certainly wrong. But the process of reasoning involved in determining what foods one is "allergic" to is the same as the one the Semai use in the selection of plant medicines. True, some of these medicines are probably worthless medically. Continually testing home remedies means, however, that the Semai are likely to discover most plants of curative value in their environment. Drug companies in Europe and America have made fortunes from cures discovered by peoples as technologically backward as the Semai. In other words, Semai-style science (or "concrete science," as some anthropologists call it) has made discoveries that eluded Euro-American science. Semai medicine should therefore not be faulted merely because it is not Euro-American medicine. One must also recognize that Semai medicine can make and probably has made considerable achievements on its own, without the benefits of a complex technology.

HOME VISITS   If self-treatment proves unsuccessful, one or more people

East Semai man wearing medicine for head and chest pains (1962).

who know appropriate spells (*jampi'*, which are usually in Malay, or *chənagɔh*, which are in Semai) may be called in. Most people who know such spells are at least a little *halaa'*. The administration of the spells varies somewhat according to the type of ailment.

For pains in the stomach, liver, or bladder, the procedure is as follows. The patient lies supine with the practitioner kneeling at his right side.[3] The practitioner clenches his right fist in front of his mouth to form a tube through which, if he is really *halaa'*, he can see *nyani'*. He blows into the tube thus formed to prepare it, whispers the *jampi'* or *chənagɔh* into it, and makes squeaky sucking noises into it to "draw out" (*tərhɔr*) the "poison" or the *nyani'*. Next, he grips the left side of the patient's waist with his left hand, extends his right arm across the patient's body, and presses his lips against his own right bicep. He draws his right hand across the patient's body, kneading strongly with his fingers and sucking squeakily at his bicep to draw out the *nyani'* or "poison." When his right hand reaches his left, he clasps his hands, raises them to eye level, blows on them, and wrings them. He repeats this procedure until he feels he has the *nyani'* or "poison" caught, then he turns away from the patient, pounds the fist holding the disease agent against a house post, claps his hands, and throws the *nyani'* or its "poison" over the wall of the house.

For missing *ruai*, the procedure is similar. The practitioner takes a whisk of magic leaves (*gərnar*), slaps them against the palm of his hand, and waves (*gar*) them over the patient's head. Next, he hisses and puts his hands on the patient's forehead to "open" it for inspection. If he thus ascertains that *ruai* is gone, he suggests holding a "sing."

Other procedures are similar to the two just described.

"SING" If home visits fail to produce a cure, the next step is to hold a two-night "sing." These "sings" take many forms, varying from place to place and occasion to occasion. They occur at night so that the *ruai gunig* will not be afraid to come. The women sit in a row along a log of firewood or house pole. Each woman has two bamboo tubes, one longer than the other. They rhythmically pound the tubes against the pole, producing a two-note background music. The *halaa'* each in turn sing their melodies against this background, often with an antiphonal reprise by the audience.

The audience consists of the patient, his immediate consanguineal kinsmen, and other people who want to take advantage of the opportunity to have their ailments treated. In the east, where the aboriginal economy still is functioning unimpaired, most of the settlement attends. The economic fragmentation of the west seems reflected in the fact that only a relatively small proportion of the population comes to the "sing."

In the house where the "sing" takes place are a "spirit perch" for the *ruai* or *kəloog* of the *gunig* and a "*halaa'* room," made of leaves and flowers, in which the *halaa'* is supposed to treat the patient. The precise type of "spirit perch" required has been revealed in a dream, usually but not necessarily in a dream of the *halaa'*. Typical west Semai "spirit perches" are small platforms hung from the rafters. East

---

[3] This description is for a right-handed practitioner. The Semai, except where under Malay influence, make no magical distinction between left and right.

Semai "spirit perches" usually are poles inserted through the floor slats and surmounted by four crosspieces that form an "X" parallel with the floor. In either case the "spirit perch" is lavishly ornamented with fragrant herbs and flowers that attract the *ruai gunig* and the roaming *ruai* of the patient or trancers. Perferably, the perch is in the center of the *"halaa'* room."

Going into a trance is crucial to a "sing." In the east the adolescent men dance until they fall like dominoes into a trance supervised by the *halaa'*. In the trance they often have to be restrained from running into the dark rain forest to rejoin their wandering *ruai*. They remain "dead," as the Semai say, until the *halaa'* sprinkles them with water from his magic whisk. In the west the *halaa'* himself may go into trance, and his *gunig* speak through him in strange, strangled voices. After the trance, the patient is treated in the *halaa'* room much as he would be treated at home, except that the *gunig* aid diagnosis and treatment. In cases of pregnancy, supernatural weakness, or the like, the patient may also be ritually bathed. If the two-night "sing" fails to cure the patient, a six-night "sing" is held.

Death

BEFORE THE FUNERAL   Sometimes all efforts at medical treatment fail, and the patient dies. His or her housemates stretch out the corpse supine on a mat with its arms at its sides. They close the eyes with a warm cloth. From this time until the burial, people worry that the body will begin to rot in the hot, wet climate. As one man said, referring to the alcohol in which we stored animal specimens, "If we could put them in medicine as you store your animals, it wouldn't matter." The housemates bathe the corpse and sprinkle it with perfume or sweet-smelling herbs to mask any odor of decay. Sometimes, especially in the case of young children, the corpse is also bathed at the graveside. If possible, the corpse is buried on the day of death, to forestall decomposition. If death occurs in the late afternoon, however, people put off the burial until the following day.

After bathing the corpse, the housemates wrap it from head to foot in new mats and the prettiest sarongs the dead person used to wear. During this swaddling people tend to fall silent or to weep. Occasionally, someone will cry out in grief. For example, an old woman watching her young grandson being swaddled might cry, "In the earth I wear this, in my house I played naked." All the emotion expressed is spontaneous; for the Semai, unlike some peoples, do not insist that everyone should pull a long face in the presence of death whether or not he is personally unhappy. After the corpse is wrapped, the people truss it to a carrying pole.

While the household is preparing the body for burial, kinsmen and neighbors of the deceased come to his house to take over routine chores like cooking and looking after the children. Men from the settlement go to other settlements to tell his kinsmen of his death. All the descendants of the deceased's grandparents should be told of the death, as well as the grandparents themselves. Because of the hurry to bury the body, some of these kinsmen may not learn of the death in time to attend the funeral. In this case, they should be on hand for the feast that takes place six nights after the funeral.

THE FUNERAL   Besides these kinsmen, all the people in the dead person's settlement should attend the funeral. Usually, however, only one or two dozen people attend, most of them kinsmen. Some people stay away because funerals depress them. People with young children often do not attend, for fear of bringing back from the grave evil influences like the "smell of death" and thus putting the child in danger. Such absences can lead to bitter feelings between members of the funeral party and the absentees.

The dead person's father, sons, and usually his brothers stay in the house with the women and the corpse. Most of the men and a few women and children go out to the cemetery, which is usually well out of sight of the settlement. Two or three men start digging the grave, while the others sit or stand around smoking and chatting. Occasionally, someone will crack a joke or engage in a little horseplay like letting the dirt thrown out of the grave fall on one of the onlookers. Although the atmosphere is not particularly happy, neither is it particularly solemn. Another set of diggers relieves the first after 15 or 20 minutes, and so forth, until the grave is dug.

The diggers first dig a broad trench 2 or 3 feet deep. The west Semai say that, if possible, the trench should run east and west so that the corpse's head can be put in the west, "where the sun dies." Within the broad trench the men dig a narrower trench about 2 feet deep, leaving ledges on both sides. The trenches should be deep, people say, so that the smell of putrefaction will not leak out. Ideally, there should be three fires at the head of the grave and three at the foot, making up the magic number of six. The underlying rationale of these fires is that fire keeps evil emanations from the grave at bay. Most of the time, however, burial parties content themselves with one or two fires.

Two men carry the swaddled body of a dead adult to the grave on a carrying pole. A father carries his dead baby in his arms. The corpse is stretched out supine in the narrower trench. This part of the ceremony seems to be the hardest for the survivors to bear. There is little or no joking or horseplay. People cry out the name of the dead person or keep repeating the kinship term they used for him, for example, "Oh, my mɘnai, oh, my mɘnai." Since the Semai say sympathy is "useless," people ignore the mourners who break down and cry. Two men roof over the narrow trench with flattened bamboo and begin to fill the grave. The roof keeps dirt from hitting the corpse's face. The corpse feels nothing, people say, but the burial party could not "bear" the idea of throwing dirt in the dead person's eyes and nose. West Semai rich enough to afford a coffin sometimes omit the roof.

When the grave is filled, the mound is smoothed off. The west Semai plant shrubs and trees around the grave. The east Semai (and formerly the west Semai as well) build a small atap lean-to over the grave to keep the rain off. Again, people say that the corpse feels nothing, but that the idea of the rain chilling the buried body of someone you liked or loved is intolerable. If necessary, a fence is put around the grave to keep animals away.

In theory, all the dead person's moveable property is put in or on the grave. One way of realizing what "high infant mortality" means is to walk through a west Semai graveyard and see the little hats and shirts, the bright plastic toys, all that the desperately poor parents could give their children. People usually break or rip the goods they put in or on the grave, so that no passerby will take them. Almost no

Carrying a corpse to the grave (East Semai, 1962).

one thinks that these goods will be of any use to the dead person. "The things rot, the people rot," one man put it. Having these possessions around, however, would call up unbearably poignant memories of the dead person. For all the strength of these feelings, an especially "daring" member of the burial party might covet some extremely valuable thing that the dead person owned, a brand new blowpipe, for example, or a beautifully ornamented quiver. In such a case, no one will object if he takes it.

There are some exceptions to the general pattern of funerals. A person who dies outdoors should be buried where he or she fell. The west Semai mark the extraordinary powers of midwives and *halaa'* by reversing the orientation of the corpse so that the head is in the east, "where the sun comes alive." An exceptionally great *halaa'* (less than one in a hundred, people say) may receive *pənasar*, "burial" above the ground, on a platform in a tall tree he has selected (east Semai) or in a small house with a raised floor (west Semai). During our fieldwork, one old west Semai *halaa'* asked for *pənasar*. After his death, however, his son and some of the older men in the settlement decided against *pənasar* because they were not sure how to go about it and because they were afraid of getting in trouble with the Malays. A person who receives *pənasar* is said to turn into a local spirit or supernatural tiger that looks after the welfare of the people in the area as the *halaa'* did in life.

AFTER THE FUNERAL With the closing of the grave, a period of danger begins for the whole community. Many Semai think that some part of the dead person, perhaps his shadow, becomes a malevolent *nyani'* called *kətmoid*. Like other *nyani'*, the *kətmoid* has no set shape. Large toads and bullfrogs may be *kətmoid*. The *kətmoid* may also be black and humanoid, with livid eyes; its arms are raised above shoulder level and stretched out to clutch people. In a symbolic expression of the total opposition between *kɔtmoid* and living people, some Semai assign *kɔtmoid* characteristics that are the reverse of human ones, like eyes in the back of its head or a habit of wearing its backbasket upside down.

Similarly, rituals to cure someone affected by *kɔtmoid* should be mirror images of rituals for ordinary *nyani'*. The most dangerous kind of *kɔtmoid* is that of a young child, especially one neglected by its parents. The parents of a recently dead young child should take ritual precautions against its *kɔtmoid* for six nights after the funeral. West Semai will bring delicacies to the grave during this period, but the east Semai usually do not put food on a grave. The people most likely to be victims of *kɔtmoid* are the dead person's parents, children, spouse, or siblings, especially if they are already sick.

To ward off the danger of *kɔtmoid,* a *halaa'* addresses the new grave, explaining that the person is dead now and should not come back to make trouble for the living. Various ritual objects are put on the grave to control its baneful influence. On the way home, the burial party carefully wash themselves to remove any trace of the smell of death, which attracts *kɔtmoid.* The members of the dead person's household then ritually purify the house of death and feast the burial party. For the rest of the day of the funeral, and sometimes for two days thereafter, the descendants of the dead person's grandparents should abstain from work, unless there is something that must be done right away.

As the evening after the funeral approaches, the Semai, especially the east Semai, begin to get nervous. *Kɔtmoid* are a common topic of conversation, and people begin to hear *kɔtmoid* moving around in the forest or even in the thatch of the house. Children are called indoors, and people start home early to arrive before dusk. In one case in which there had been two deaths in a week in a nearby settlement, an east Semai man's mother-in-law actually asked to sleep in the same room with him, being afraid to sleep by herself. He was shocked, but agreed that under the circumstances he had to let her do it. On the other hand, not everyone takes *kɔtmoid* seriously. For example, in the same east Semai settlement, three adolescent boys effectively broke the tension by running through the settlement one evening shrieking, *"Kɔtmoid! Kɔtmoid!"* and laughing hysterically. Even the people who believed in *kɔtmoid* thought the performance was amusing.

Formerly, the Semai used to abandon a settlement after someone died in it. Even now, after two or three deaths in fairly quick succession, people will move away from the place of death. For example, most of the people from across the river moved into our settlement after the deaths described in the preceding paragraph. The rationale given for this move was that *kɔtmoid* cannot cross water. For this reason, the best place for a graveyard is across a stream from the settlement. The east Semai also say that, if someone in a small house dies, the survivors move out and burn the house down.

Although there are always *kɔtmoid* around, the six nights after a funeral are the most dangerous. On the seventh day the funeral party gathers again at the house of deceased for a feast. At this time the west Semai usually mark the grave by putting a rectangular wooden frame on top of it and filling the frame with earth or, if the money is available, with cement.

If the deceased was an infant too young to be "a real person," this second funerary feast marks the end of the mourning period. Otherwise, close kinsmen and people from the dead person's settlement should continue to refrain from singing, dancing, wearing face paint, and playing musical instruments (especially wind instruments, which are said to resemble the voice of *kɔtmoid*). The duration of this mourning period varies from one to two months. It tends to be shorter in the west than in the east, and apparently it used to be longer in the east than it is now. The end of this period is marked by a "sing," with songs based on the theme that "the agreed time is passed, the agreement fulfilled."

Most Semai are willing to talk about life after death, but they usually volunteer the information that they do not believe in it. Some people find the idea ludicrous: "How can a person die twice?" Others are more cynical: "People die, animals die, it's the same thing." Most people profess ignorance: "I suppose the *kɔloog* goes back where it came from. Who knows where that is?" Some of the more thoughtful west Semai are willing to entertain the idea that the *kɔloog* returns to "Grandparent" (*Jɔnang*), a deity unknown in the east and probably of Malay and/or Christian origin. My impression is that these people refrain from rejecting these ideas out of hand not so much because they find the ideas intrinsically convincing but because they suspect that Malays and Christians, both vastly more powerful people than the Semai, may have access to sources of information as yet unavailable to the Semai.

For all their fear of *kɔtmoid* and their skepticism about life after death, the Semai find the fact that they live where their ancestors are buried emotionally satisfying. People constantly refer to this fact when complaining about their relocation during the Communist rebellion. Durian, an old east Semai man, put it this way:

> This is what we call our "traditional land." Perhaps we don't build a settlement, but we bury our children here. I buried my father in this earth; I buried my grandchild; I buried my elder brother. When I die, my wife will bury me in this earth. After that she'll pound rice, give it to the people and go wherever she will. All of us have always been buried here from the beginning of time. When I die, my children will replace me. When they die, my grandchildren will replace them. I don't want to live in another place. Next time, if war comes, tell them to let us stay here. So we die here. It doesn't matter. I don't want always to be moving upstream and downstream. I just want to stay here.

Underlying Attitudes

SKEPTICISM The Semai attitude toward the matters discussed in this chapter is skeptical, eclectic, and pragmatic. Understanding this attitude is crucial to understanding Semai thought.

Semai faith in the efficacy of these concepts and rituals is tempered by a great skepticism. An east Semai man will describe in great detail how the *ruai gunig* weakens the end of a bamboo tube used for ritual bathing so that the *halaa'* can crack it open with his bare hands after the lights come on again, but the informant adds, "Probably the *halaa'* hits it with a machete while the lights are out." Similarly, a west Semai *halaa'* whose patients have died despite his *jampi'* may conclude that his *jampi'* are no good any more. People who have been advised by a *halaa'* after a "sing" to give up certain foods will "test" small portions of the forbidden foods to see whether in fact they get sicker. Dreams, so important in the diagnosis and treatment of disease, are generally said to be unreliable. One can only really rely on a dream that has recurred three times.

As might be expected, the atmosphere of a "sing" is not at all reverent. In the east, where other types of entertainment are few, "sings," are sometimes held just for fun, with the lights left on. Even when the "sing" is to cure the sick, adolescents will take the opportunity of darkness to flirt with each other. A *halaa'* will exhort his *gunig* to hurry up and cooperate because he is tired and wants to go to bed. In short, the Semai attitude toward the concepts they associate with health and disease is one of careful skepticism, not awe.

ECLECTICISM   The Semai have great respect for the "wisdom" of other peoples. For instance, the west Semai have recently become exposed to diseases like leprosy and cholera for which there are no traditional cures, since the diseases are unknown in the rain forest fastnesses. These diseases, they say, are due to "sea *nyani'*." One has to use Malay or Chinese magic against such unfamiliar diseases. Malay amulets and house charms are in wide use among the west Semai for the same reasons. Similarly, western medicine has had an impact on the west Semai. In the old days (and still in the east) the Semai recognized a condition in which the spleen was swollen, a condition which Euro-American doctors attribute usually to malaria. For the Semai "spleen sickness" was due to *nyani'* and/or eating too many sweet or acidic foods. The treatment was *jampi'* or "sing," followed by abstinence from sweet foods. Now, however, the west Semai acknowledge a second disease, *nya'ni' malaria,* which is due to germs and should be treated in a hospital. The important thing about this recognition, however, is that it does not preclude recognizing and treating "spleen sickness" by the traditional methods.

In other words, the Semai accept new ideas readily without giving up the old ones. Recognition of *nya'ni' malaria* does not imply giving up the traditional concept of "spleen sickness." There are Semai who regard themselves as simultaneously Methodists and Baha'i, without having abandoned any of their traditional beliefs. The idea that one sort of knowledge implicitly excludes another is alien to the Semai. Thus, they are not uneasy about describing *ruai* as simultaneously tiny man, bird, and child. *Nyani'* are, similarly, both invisible and visible. One east Semai man was accused of burying corpses so close to another settlement that the *kətmoid* came across the river and haunted people there. He argued (successfully) in his own defense that, first there is no such thing as a *kətmoid* and, second, the *kətmoid* could not cross the river. In short, while Euro-Americans tend to think in "either/or" categories, the Semai seem to think in terms of "both . . . and."

PRACTICALITY   This skepticism and eclecticism seem to rest on a basic practicality in Semai thinking. The question of where *nyani'* go when they are not molesting human beings is of no importance, because people only worry about *nyani'* when they are causing trouble. If possible, a new concept is made to fit with the old. For example, the Semai say that one kind of lung disease is due to *nya'ni' pənali',* which attacks people who have mixed together certain sorts of food that should be eaten separately. (Sometimes they say that the mere mixture of foods has this effect without the intervention of a *nyani'.*) X-rays of victims of this disease often showed the characteristic shadows of tuberculosis infection. Semai shown these photographs concluded that a third contributing factor in the disease is the "steam" arising from such mixed foods, as attested by the smoke visible in the x-rays. They also recognized a new disease, *nya'ni' tiibii* (tuberculosis), which was caused by "germs" and had similar effects.

Even if a concept does not fit neatly with old concepts, the Semai will accept it if it *works,* explains something or is the basis of successful action. If a *halaa'* fails, it is because his proven powers have been weakened. If a patient recovers after a "sing," his recovery is due to the "sing." If he recovers after a visit to a hospital, his recovery is due to the killing of the "germs" of the disease. Since the Semai usually do not entrust their stick to *mai* in hospitals until they are very ill indeed, the recovery rates for either sort of treatment are about the same. Thus, there is in Semai experience nothing to force a choice between *nyani'* causation and "germ" causation. Both "germs" and *nyani'* are invisible to the Semai, although *nyani'* appear in dreams. Sometimes hospitals or "sings" produce cures, sometimes not. Neither is conclusively more effective than the other.

In Euro-American science, as noted in Chapter 3, the rule is that when two explanations both sufficiently account for the same set of facts, then the simpler explanation is the better. For example, for centuries the only reason for preferring Copernican to Ptolemaic astronomy was that Copernicus' theory was simpler. There is, however, no way of telling whether nature itself actually follows this rule of simplicity, this principle of parsimony. In fact, almost everyone has had the feeling that "things are more camplicated than we think they are," and a large segment of Euro-American society complains that "science" takes the "life" out of what it studies. In short, the principle of parsimony does not force itself on an observer. Semai science effectively ignores it in favor of practical beliefs that lead to actions which, the Semai think, bring results. This lack of parsimony makes Semai "science" an immensely complex, almost baroque system of overlapping and often mutually incompatible concepts and explanations.

This sort of thinking seems to be characteristic of technologically "primitive" peoples and has been labelled the science of the concrete. Nevertheless, there is nothing especially "primitive" about thinking this way. It is probably the mode of thought of most Euro-Americans, even of scientists in their unguarded moments. In fact, Semai *halaa'* and Euro-American doctors use the same sort of explanations for their failures, for example, "the disease was too far advanced to treat." In neither case do people abandon their concepts of medicine simply because they do not always succeed. Anyone who believes in atoms knows that a table top is mostly empty space, but he can at the same time think of it as "solid wood." The Semai can equally well think of *ruai* in three different ways, simultaneously hold both the germ and *nyani'* theories of disease, and the like. The Semai are, perhaps, better able to tolerate holding mutually incompatible ideas than Euro-Americans are, but such ability is not unique to Semai.

10

Dangerous Situations: Pregnancy, Childbirth, and Menstruation

T HE SEMAI regard certain physiological conditions as dangerous. Infancy and disease, already discussed, are two of these states. Other important dangerous states include pregnancy, recuperation after childbirth, and menstruation. In many societies these three states are hedged in by strict taboos with specified supernatural penalties for breaking the taboos. Superficially, Semai society seems similar. Closer investigation shows, however, first, that there are great differences between east and west Semai attitudes toward these states; second, that people in the same settlement often do not agree on just what the "taboos" are or what the "penalties" for violation are; and, third, that people often ignore the "taboos."

In the first part of this chapter the Semai response to these three physiological states is described. In the second, the way in which Semai "taboos" work is analyzed.

Dangerous Conditions

PREGNANCY   When a Semai woman misses her menstrual period, she or her husband usually calls a midwife (*bidat*) to palpate her stomach and to tell whether she is really pregnant. These midwives are, typically, older women who have had many children themselves and are therefore thoroughly familiar with the course of pregnancy and childbirth. They are normally "a little" *halaa'* because they have to deal with such mysterious dangers of this period as *nyani'*. West Semai explain that midwives must be somewhat *halaa'* in order to seek aid from the "First Midwife" who dwells in the uppermost tier of the seven-layered heavens and from the six other Midwives in the other tiers. Since six is the magic number of the Semai and seven of the Malays, there is some reason to think that the notion of the "Seven Midwives" was originally Malay.

At some time during the course of the pregnancy the woman and her midwife should be ceremonially bathed in water made fragrant by magical plants, preferably at a "sing." This ritual is to assure that the child will come out as easily as the water flows from its container and that the mother and her midwife will be supernaturally "cool," that is, healthy.

Cravings for "sweet" or "acidic" foods are common during pregnancy. Frustrating such cravings would put the woman into *punan*. Nevertheless, there is a wide variety of foods which she should avoid, and the east Semai recognize another set of foods which neither she nor her husband should eat. Both she and her husband should also avoid any activity that might "block the womb," like eating canned food, or that might "twist" the birth canal, like wringing out a cloth. As the pregnancy advances, the woman should exert herself less and less. She eventually stops going out into the heat of the midafternoon. By the time she is almost ready to give birth she has even stopped cooking. She still has sexual relations with her husband, however.

The extent to which the parents-to-be follow these restrictions varies widely. There is, of course, no way of forcing people to observe them, for that would be *punan*. A husband may complain, for example, that his wife "eats just anything," but "What can I do? It's her affair." The strongest pressure he can bring is to suggest that her carelessness about what she eats means that she does not love her unborn child. But he would be "ashamed" to accuse her of such callousness to her face. To her husband's complaining the wife may respond that nothing bad will happen, because she feels in good health, or because she eats just a little of the forbidden food, or because she has had children with no trouble before, or because of a combination of these reasons.

CHILDBIRTH AND AFTERWARDS   Childbirth usually occurs at home. In traditional Semai houses, which have slatted floors, there is no problem about disposing of the discharge, which goes through the floor. In the Malay-style plank-floored houses owned by some west Semai, childbirth usually occurs in the kitchen, where the floor is left slatted for easy disposal of debris.

Kinsmen and neighbors drop in during the course of the labor pains to see how things are progressing and to bring food to the household. Men tend to be somewhat uneasy about the whole process because of "all that blood," but they are allowed to visit if they want to. When the pains begin to come close together, the midwife and a *halaa'* arrive. If the birth is difficult other *halaa'* may be called in. The job of the *halaa'* is to call on his *gunig* for aid. Other people present recite any appropriate "spells" they happen to know. From time to time the husband or the midwife kneads the woman's belly or sprinkles her with fragrant water to keep her supernaturally "cool." The women of the household or close kinsmen of the couple keep busy pounding medicinal herbs for the *halaa'*, preparing food for the visitors, and warming water for the washing that immediately precedes and follows the birth.

At last, if all goes well, the midwife eases the child out and puts it on a cloth. She has warm stones sent in from the kitchen and sends a bystander out for fresh leaves to be tied with the stones around the mother's waist "to heal her womb." The midwife then washes her hands in warm water, cuts the umbilical cord, and kneads the mother's stomach to bring out the afterbirth, which should be saved for later disposal in a place safe from *nyani'*. Finally, she washes the baby in warm water and puts it to nurse at her own breast. This "suckling" serves merely to symbolize the strength of the bond between the midwife and child, for the midwife's breasts usually have no milk.

The Semai say that the scent of the discharge attracts *nyani'*, especially the dreadful "bird *nyani'*" that usually take the form of seductive maidens euphemistically referred to as "the longhaired ones." A trace of the discharge in the river will attract "water *nyani'*." Similarly, care must be taken to keep the baby's umbilical cord from falling to the ground. On the other hand, as one man observed after the stump of his baby's cord had fallen through the slats and been eaten by a chicken, "If you can't get it, you can't get it. It's no use worrying." The east Semai say that until a few years ago they used to hang a small earth-covered platform beneath the place of birth to absorb the discharge. West Semai husbands fence in the area of ground below the place where the baby will be born with pieces of roofing and set a piece of iron in the center, because iron is supposed to repel *nyani'* (a Malay belief).

For six (east) or seven (west) days after the birth the mother, midwife, and baby should stay in the room where the birth occurred. This is often impractical in the smaller west Semai houses, and the midwife goes home, but returns frequently. In the larger east Semai communal houses people set up temporary partitions to mark off the area of the main floor where the birth occurred. People try to avoid physical contact with mother, baby, or midwife. One reason given is that they might carry the *nyani'*-attracting smell of the discharge outdoors with them. Warm leaves, warm stones and/or warm ashes wrapped in leaves are tied around the mother's waist to "warm her womb," a Malay custom. The mother and the midwife bathe each other and the child several times daily with warm water from special containers.

Even after this period of seclusion, the tie between midwife and child remains strong. If the midwife falls sick, the Semai say that the child is likely to fall sick. For this reason people prefer fat (that is, healthy) midwives to thin and sickly ones. Conversely, if the child falls sick, it is a sign that the midwife's powers have weakened and become *jah* (see Chapter 5). Finally, if the mother does not look after the child properly, the midwife's *ruai* will spirit the child's *ruai* away. In any of these three cases the mother, midwife, and child should ritually bathe together.

The mother decides for herself when she feels like going back to heavy work, but people expect her to take it easy for a month or so while her womb is supposed to be healing. In the east husband and wife should sleep at least two arms' lengths apart immediately after the child is born. As the time passes the husband edges closer and closer until, when the baby can crawl on all fours and if the wife is in good health, the couple again sleep side by side with the baby between them. In smaller houses people usually ignore this precaution. For a couple of years postpartum they should not copulate with each other, although the husband may at this time take advantage of his *mɔnai* relationships. The east Semai explain that this abstinence among other things permits a couple to space their children so that they can give adequate care to each. In the west, where the *mɔnai* relationship is sexually much less free, the period of abstinence is much shorter. It should last forty-four days, as it does among the Malays, but as one man asked, "Who can wait that long?"

After a birth, the mother, and in some instances the father as well, should avoid eating certain foods. The west Semai avoid about the same proportion of foods as the east Semai, but most western avoidances last for a significantly shorter period. Similarly, the east Semai father should restrict his diet much more extensively than the west Semai one. Although people usually disagree about which avoidance protects whom from what, many of the avoidances practiced by the mother alone are said to be for her own welfare and many of those practiced by both parents are for the welfare of the child.

Again, there is a great deal of individual variation about observing these precautions. If mother and child are healthy, the duration of the food avoidances is relatively short. If either falls sick the precautions may drag on for months or even years. Many precautions are explicitly tied to the child's development so that some stop when it crawls, some when it toddles, and so forth. A sickness that retards the child's development thus tends to lengthen the period of restrictions. As during pregnancy, there is much testing of dangerous foods, especially by people who have had several children without any trouble before.

MENSTRUATION Semai women normally menstruate once every twenty-eight days. They say that "fat" (that is, healthy) women have longer periods than "thin" (that is, unhealthy) ones. The east Semai refer to menstruation by a series of euphemisms like "bleeding." They also aver that first menses are sometimes due to initial sexual intercourse, subsequent menses being the discharge from this incurable wound. In the west, where people usually do not have sexual intercourse until two or three years past puberty, people say menstruation "just happens."

Menstruating women should not take long walks, do hard work, or overexert themselves, although healthy women usually ignore these precautions. They should sleep a little further away from their husbands than usual and should not engage in sexual intercourse. While bathing, menstruating women usually undress separately from other women in order to hide the leaf or pad of cloth with which they staunch the flow. The Semai say that menstrual fluid is "like fish poison" and that if a menstruating woman joins in poisoning fish she will turn into a tiger.[1]

A menstruating east Semai woman supposedly should leave her house only to defecate or urinate, bathing being in theory prohibited at this time. Only girls menstruating for the first or second time pay much attention to this rule. She should also cook and eat separately from other people, and often does. There are many foods which she should not share with other people, a common explanation being that eating them might cause cramps. There are other foods which she should not eat at all.

Menstruating west Semai women should cook only for themselves, but they usually continue to cook for others. People say that copulating with a menstruating woman is "dirty," but unlikely to have ill effects. There are very few food avoidances.

Once again, there is a great deal of individual variation, both about the reasons these precautions should be observed and about actually observing them.

---

[1] Such transformations are also part of Semai animal lore. Striped frogs reportedly change into tigers and vice versa, eels into cobras, and so forth. Some of the food restrictions that a menstruating woman should observe are explained as precautions against such transformations, although many Semai doubt that they ever occur.

The Nature of Semai Precautions

The precautions that the Semai may or may not take during these dangerous periods are not "taboos" in the sense that anthropologists usually use the word. No one enforces them. Enough people ignore them without any trouble to make it clear to the Semai that there is no automatic supernatural penalty for doing so. Because "daring" (bərani') people get away with ignoring the precautions, it is difficult to get a clear account of what *will* happen as the result of ignoring them, although people may retrospectively decide that a certain misfortune *has* happened because a certain precaution was not taken, as in the case of disease. In short, like Semai concepts of disease, Semai notions of these precautions are closely bound to specific personal experiences. They serve to explain an experience and to provide a way to prevent its recurrence.

A Semai determines whether or not to take these precautions on the basis of his personal history. If a person is approaching a dangerous situation like childbirth for the first time, he or she tends to be especially careful. A person who has gone through the same situation two or three times without any ill effects is apt to be a little "daring." Explaining a certain precaution, such an experienced person often expresses skepticism about the rationale: "They say she'll turn into a tiger, but I don't believe it." If, however, something goes wrong—if, say, a menstruating woman has cramps—then it is always possible to take the suggested precautions and thus to rest secure in the knowledge that one has done what people say is needful to prevent a recurrence of the unpleasantness.

Some of the recommended precautions almost certainly do have the effect the Semai claim for them and do avert certain dangers. Others almost certainly do not. The important thing is that the Semai think that they do. At first glance some of the precautions seem to be fanciful. This apparent fancifulness is partially due to the explanations people give for taking the precautions. It should be remembered, however, that there is great disagreement about these explanations. This situation seems to come about because of the practicality of Semai thinking. The crucial issue for the Semai is to avert danger, not to speculate about just what dangers a specific act averts. The suggested precautions are guides to action, neither "religious" rules nor the products of speculation. The rationale for a particular action is the product of the action, not its cause. In other words, a Semai woman does not really avoid eating venison because she thinks it will turn her into a deer, or make her baby grow horns, or the like. Whatever her beliefs about the effects of eating venison may be, they serve mainly to rationalize her action.

If these rationalizations are left aside, patterns appear that the Semai themselves do not make explicit. For example, the more dangerous a person feels a given situation to be, the more foods he or she stops eating. Furthermore, a person whose experience with the situation has been uneventful will avoid only the flesh of the largest animals, whereas a less secure person will avoid not only those meats but also the flesh of smaller animals (see Chapter 3). It is as if the Semai were engaged in a sort of unconscious gamble with danger. On the one hand, a person wants to be able to eat as many kinds of food as possible, to have a minimum number of restrictions on his or her freedom of action. On the other hand, the person also wants to run as few risks as possible, and he or she supposedly reduces risks by giving up certain sorts of foods and restricting his or her activities. The actual behavior of the person at any given time is the product of these two opposing tendencies. In brief, the precautions are not to be understood as rules that constrain behavior. Like the other "rules" of Semai society, they provide, rather, a framework within which the individual Semai can work out his own gamble with danger. The rationales merely validate the gamble.

11

Present and Future

Present

THE CHARACTERISTIC of Semai society that strikes most outsiders immediately is the emphasis on nonviolence. The concept of *punan* transforms almost any interference with another person's affairs into prohibited violence. The result is a rather remarkable degree of individual autonomy, limited mainly by strongly internalized controls over "violent" impulses.

This autonomy, however, is not won without cost. Apparently the individual Semai tends to feel essentially isolated from his fellows. The emphasis on non-violence seems to lead to a fear or suspicion of *mai*. This suspicion makes it hard for the Semai to organize themselves to deal profitably as a group with other Malaysians. It also tends to make them dubious about the intentions of the Malaysian government toward them, although those intentions usually aim at betterment of the conditions under which the Semai live. The techniques of dealing with *mai* by avoidance and deception, historically so successful, now often operate to the disadvantage of the Semai.

Within Semai society few rules constrain the action of the individual. The kinship system lets him emphasize those relationships that he finds personally satisfactory, while ignoring the rest. The qualifications for the important statuses in Semai society are flexible enough to leave great room for individual maneuver. The main external control on a person's freedom of action is public opinion: "The only authority here is embarrassment." If public opinion goes against a man he has always the option of moving to another settlement.

In the same way Semai thought is flexible enough to leave leeway for individual maneuver. What seems at first to be vagueness or confusion actually makes it possible to tie concepts to specific personal experiences. What seem to be rules that people often disobey turn out to be guideposts that the individual can exploit to suit his personal needs.

Future

This flexible and personalized society is gradually coming under the influence of a relatively rigid and relatively impersonal bureaucratic state. True, there are still Semai in the east who have never heard of Malaysia and who are not sure that the British have left. But the west Semai, who probably represent what the east Semai will become, are alert to the greater society that is beginning to envelop them. Greater ease of transportation and greater contact with non-Semai are making the west Semai more conscious of themselves as an ethnic group. They have already made abortive attempts to organize themselves for positive political action, and it seems likely that such attempts will eventually succeed.

The Semai will probably resist any attempt to amalgamate them to the rest of the Malayan population. The poses of passive acquiescence or·obdurate stupidity are merely poses. They mask a stubborn determination to preserve individual and collective Semai autonomy in the face of what the Semai take to be an overwhelmingly more powerful, violent, and inimical world. In the east the sole function of the largest political groupings is to maintain this covert defiance of the non-Semai world. Even in the west, where the Semai are becoming culturally more and more like rural Malays, people strongly reject the idea of embracing Islam and thus legally "becoming Malays." They respect Islam, but say that they could not stand its food taboos nor the practice of circumcision. If anything, increasing awareness of themselves as Semai is increasing this resistance to assimilation.

As a tiny minority of the population of Malaysia the Semai have special problems, especially with regard to land. The Malaysian government does not and cannot acknowledge Semai claims to vast areas of the interior of the peninsula. The loss of "traditional lands" is now and probably will continue to be a very sore point in the years to come. In the past the colonial government sometimes took or sold Semai land without even being aware that the Semai claimed it. Unscrupulous private individuals cheated the Semai of the land in which the ancestors of the Semai were buried. Since independence, with the establishment of the Department of Aborigines, the situation has improved somewhat. The government is becoming more aware of Semai claims to land and is moving toward compensating and resettling displaced Semai, while guarding them from exploitation by private persons.

The Department of Aborigines is an impressively well-staffed and forward-looking institution. It has been active in instituting development schemes among the Semai. The medical services provided by the Department are probably superior to those available to American Indians. Liaison between the Department and the Semai is still shaky, but the recently instituted policy of hiring Semai to work with Semai should improve this situation. So should the policy of staffing the higher echelons of the Department with trained anthropologists.

Despite their small numbers and economic weakness, the Semai have managed for the most part to avoid the painful experience of being forcibly subjected to the rule of another people. For all their gentleness, they remain strongly independent and resentful of any attempt by *mai* to force them into any activity. They have always been surprisingly successful at maintaining themselves in the face of pressures from more powerful and sometimes hostile peoples. Semai society is flexible and resilient. It continually changes and adapts to new situations, but its traditional openness to new ideas has in large part prevented this process from being as disruptive as it has been for many peoples. Semai culture retains its vitality, and there is no real reason to think it will stop doing so.

12

Living and Working
with the Semai

Introduction[1]

At the outset, I want to make two points. First, the following account emphasizes our field experience more than our field techniques. Many cultural anthropologists tend to romanticize fieldwork to the point of making a fetish out of it, claiming that their field experience gives them insights into the nature of human society that no other discipline can provide. This insight, they contend, stems from the fact that anthropological fieldwork is an intensely personal experience. The difficulty they have in communicating the nature of this experience makes their colleagues in other fields rather suspicious of anthropology's claim to superior insight. I am suspicious of it myself. Nevertheless, I want to stress how intensely personal the fieldwork experience was for me and Ruth, then my wife.

[1] I want to thank Drs. Edwin S. Hall, Rodney Needham, and Thomas R. Williams, as well as a host of students and friends, for reading and commenting on this chapter.

Robert Dentan burning the fur off a monkey (1963).

One reason fieldwork has this character, I think, is that, unlike other "social scientists," an anthropologist in a remote community is doing research all day, every day. This sort of total immersion is quite different from, say, getting some questionnaires filled out and then going home for a beer. For about a year and a half, our "home" was with the Semai, and there was no beer around. For much of that time, the only people we had to talk with were Semai. Communicating with them thus became a tremendous personal need. Our social life and our research were inextricably intertwined.

Another reason our fieldwork had this personal character was that, at first, we had a hard time just getting along from day to day among people in whose terms we were weird and barely comprehensible outsiders with the social and technical skills of a Semai four-year-old. This initial social situation produced in us a psychological condition anthropologists call "culture shock." We felt depressed, incompetent, unattractive, and very lonely. I can easily understand the response of the great anthropologist Malinowski (1967: 261) when he writes in his field diary that one trivial frustrating incident "drives me to a state of white rage and hatred of bronze-colored skin, combined with depression, a desire to 'sit down and cry,' and a furious longing *'to get out of this.'* For all that, I decide to resist and work today—*'business as usual,'* despite everything." Although Ruth and I were physiologically and emotionally adult, we were to the Semai socially children. We had to learn Semai ways in the manner that children in any society have to come to grips with the often incomprehensible demands and expectations of adults. We made the same sorts of *faux pas* and went through the same sorts of traumas that children do while growing up. In many ways we never did "grow up" in Semai terms. To take a simple instance, Ruth was never able to pound our clothes dry against a rock the way the other women did. The women washing clothes with her would almost always comment, "Oh, Ruth, you're doing that just like a child." After a while, that sort of remark gets pretty hard to take.

Since from the Semai point of view we were always rather inept, we could not help feeling very grateful and very affectionate toward them when they came to accept us as people much like other people. For example, Ruth, who normally prides herself on the excellence of her cooking, still recalls how delighted she was the first time someone said of one of her meals, "You know, this tastes just as if any other woman in the settlement had cooked it." Similarly, we were very moved on a visit to a ceremony in another settlement when a man from our home settlement explained to some wary "spirits" that we were perfectly acceptable people who "speak our language, eat our food and live in one of our houses. They are of our people," he said, "just like us."

In short, whether or not our fieldwork gave us superior insights, it did not *feel* like doing research in any of the disciplines related to anthropology. We think that we understand ourselves better as a result of living with the Semai.

We also feel that it left us changed people and that the change was for the better.

It is primarily this intensely personal impact of fieldwork that makes me regret not having kept a diary in the field. The long letters that Ruth and I wrote to our families are poor substitutes for a diary. As an anthropologist, I probably would have understood the Semai better and sooner if I had forced myself to analyze my responses to them on a daily basis. More importantly (to me), as a human being, I think that keeping a diary would have helped me

East Semai woman winnowing rice.

understand the things that were happening to and within me. My regret about this omission is deepened by reading Malinowski's diary. He attempts to deal consciously with the torment of trying to communicate with people of a wholly alien background. As one of the remarkably few perceptive reviews of his diary (Gallagher 1967:26) concludes, without this sort of torment one's results "are more than just possibly liable to be piffle."

This confession of one of my errors leads to the second point I want to make. I went into the field as a tyro. Mulling over the data Ruth and I collected, I recognize that we made mistakes, both of omission and commission. Although space does not permit my "confessions of ignorance and failure" to be as extensive as Malinowski's (1935 I:452–482), I mention some of these mistakes later on. I do so not out of masochism, but because ethnographers sometimes omit such a list of errors, thus inadvertently giving the unwary reader the impressions that their accounts are definitive, the results of perfect techniques perfectly applied.

I am a firm believer in the British pattern of fieldwork, in which one goes into the field, collects one's data, goes home to examine and think about these data, and then returns to the field with a clear knowledge of one's earlier mistakes and a resolve not to repeat them. In this sense, I am currently only halfway through studying the Semai. I really must go back.

In another sense, however, I have barely begun. Anthropologists often find themselves referring to a people among whom they have lived as "my people." To a large extent, the phrase is merely a sign of affection for the people who came to accept and like one, an affection made deeper by the initial experience of culture shock. For a few anthropologists, however, "my people" carries an ugly connotation of personal ownership. I think wanting to reserve for oneself all research on a given people stems from a fear that one's own observations or interpretations may be in error. Fortunately, most anthropologists, including myself, feel that a restudy of "their" people is vital precisely to uncover such errors, as well as to provide new data. Since coming back to the United States, Ruth and I have not only encouraged people who want to study the Semai but also have tried to recruit people to do such studies. I try to keep in fairly close touch with people who are working with Semai, so that I can learn more about the Semai and so that the people in the field can get from me information that I have not yet published. It seems to me that such activities are such a logical extension of our fieldwork that they might be called "fieldwork from afar" or "fieldwork by proxy."

Entering the Field

SELECTING A PEOPLE

The problem we set out to investigate was why people the world over fail to make continuous use of foods potentially available to them. Everywhere that I know of, people subject themselves to food taboos or regard some things as unfit for human consumption. Since we intended to do a statistical analysis of variations in these food avoidances, we need to find a people who had a wide assortment of potential foods from which to choose. This consideration suggested that the people should live in tropical rain forest, because that environment usually embraces a wide variety of plants and animals. For the same reason, we decided to live in two communities in order to find out what variations there might be in food avoidances between two settlements that had a common cultural background. Finally, we wanted to study a relatively isolated people, since we felt that food avoidances might be responses to local ecology, and we hoped to avoid the problem of avoidances introduced from outside that ecology.

Originally, we settled on Indonesia as the place for our work, mainly because we had several Indonesian friends who were willing to help us gain entrée into the area. Unfortunately, during the year I was taking an intensive course in the Indonesian language, official relations between Indonesia and the United States deteriorated to the point that the Indonesian Embassy refused to issue us visas for more than three months' residence. One of the many unpleasant aspects of the present nightmarish world situation is that, while all the major world nations are deliberately or inadvertently committing cultural genocide on the ethnic minorities within their borders, anthropologists are often forbidden entrance to record these vanishing and unique styles of human living.

At any rate, we then decided to try to get into Malaya (now part of the Federation of Malaysia), since the national language there is very similar to Indonesian. We received visas with no trouble, and, when it became clear that we would have to extend our stay, the renewal of the visas took only a few minutes. It seems appropriate to say here that many anthropological grants set aside funds for "emoluments" (read: "bribes"). We received as much cooperation from Malayan officials at every level of government as anyone could ask. In the entire course of our research the only person to indicate in any way the slightest interest in an "emolument" was an American in New York City, which was also the only place anything was stolen from us.

The next step was to write a grant proposal, which we submitted to the Ford Foundation. After being awarded the grant, I went to the American Museum of Natural History and to Peabody Museum at Yale University, where I was given funds to collect artifacts. Later on, both of the first two institutions renewed our grants.

I then tried to get in touch with anthropologists who had worked with Malayan aborigines. At first, it seemed that most of them were dead. Luckily, one of the living ones, Rodney Needham, was passing through New York at the time. He agreed to meet with me. We drank beer and talked about the various problems of doing fieldwork in Malaysia, the kind of equipment needed, and so forth. He also kindly gave me a list of people in Malaya and Singapore who might be helpful to us. We wrote these people, explaining our project, giving our estimated time of arrival, and asking if we could talk with them. Their responses were, as we came to expect in Malaya, uniformly positive.

PARTICIPANT OBSERVATION AND THE EQUIPMENT PROBLEM

To explain our decision to follow Dr. Needham's advice and take along as little equipment as possible requires jumping ahead a little and explaining our decision to use a field technique called "participant observation," that is, to live as much like the local people as possible. There are two main reasons we wanted to use this technique. One was that we hoped to "learn by doing," even when "doing" meant making mistakes. For example, I do not think that I would ever have understood the economics of food distribution among the Semai if we had not participated so fully in the system that I twice got into hot water for breaking its usually unspoken rules. In one case, a close Semai friend of mine named Stump had loaded himself down with supplies from our limited stock. I told him that I would appreciate his waiting a week or so before taking any more. For the next couple of months he refused to look at me, speak to me, or enter our house, although he would come up on the porch and, with his eyes averted from me, talk to Ruth. I finally figured out that my offense was in overtly calculating the amount of food my friend took, thus hurting him deeply and completely fouling up part of a system of exchanges where values are never explicitly calculated. Similarly, I reflexively said "Thank you," but informants had told me that saying "good!" (bɔr) was the Semai equivalent of saying "Thank you," and I made a point of using the word. Finally, after one of these "Thank you's," a friend moistened his thumb and made the ritual "rubbing away" gesture the Semai use to erase evil. "What's the matter with you?" he asked. "Aren't we friends?" My error in this case involved both acting as if I did not expect him to give me things whenever he could and also seeming to feel obligated to him. In a sense, I was violating his personal integrity by implying that he was making the gift in order to get a response from me instead of out of a simple desire to give me something. My response was incompatible with the traditional Semai exchange system, but I only found that out by virtue of the blunders I made trying to participate in it.

The other reason we wanted to do participant observation was that we wanted to fade into the background, so that people (1) would feel free to behave in front of us the way they did when no outsiders were present and (2) would confide in us as freely as in anyone else. We were afraid that if people thought of us as "outsiders" they would tell us whatever they thought we wanted to hear and would conceal anything intimate or anything of which they thought we might disapprove. It turned out that both these tendencies were especially strong among the Semai. They distrust outsiders (mai) so much that they use a special slang to conceal what they are talking about in the presence of an outsider who is familiar enough with them to have picked up a smattering of their language. They feel that most outsiders regard them as stupid savages, and they play "stupid savage" for an outsider, thus at one fell swoop giving the visitor what they think he expects, amusing themselves and each other, and exploiting his stereotype of them in order to avoid cooperating with him.

Finally, we hoped that participant observation would prevent people's thinking of us as "recorders." People tend to get a little nervous when they think their actions or words are being recorded. For example, at first, when we tried to take pictures, people would rush into their houses to put on their best clothes—shoes, bras, long pants, and other garments almost never worn in the normal course of affairs. They would then arrange themselves into a grim, stiff group, glowering at the camera the way people do in late Victorian family photographs. After a while, as people got more familiar with us and the camera, they began (with some encouragement from us) to ham it up in front of the camera. When at last we had finally faded into the background, we were able to get unposed shots. The difficulties we had with photographs illustrate the problem we faced in deciding what equipment to bring into the field.

Every piece of field equipment that is "exotic" from the viewpoint of the local people sets one off as an outsider and makes manifest one's role as an observer and recorder. Even such a relatively unobtrusive thing as a small notebook can cause difficulties. One time, for instance, we were recording a ceremony in which a man was serving as the vehicle through which "spirits" could speak. We were strangers to most of the people in the settlement, although we had several friends there who explained that we were really just like Semai. The rest of the people were too polite to voice their suspicion of us directly, but it was quite clear that the "spirits" were expressing the feelings of the general community when they asked, "If the hearts of these two people are so good, why are they always writing in those little books?"

We therefore took into the field only what we thought to be absolutely necessary recording equipment: notebooks, file cards, ballpoint pens, a variety of forms and questionnaires, a 35 mm. still camera, a tape recorder, and a 16 mm. movie camera. In retrospect, I think we took too much. The tape recorder was fun for us and the Semai, when it was working. It was never working very long, however, because small creatures would get into it to eat the rubber parts, and the internal mechanisms were always getting jammed up by the bodies of the cockroaches, which tried to make the machine their home. It is possible to get "tropicalized" tape recorders that are less vulnerable than ours was, but such machines are very expensive and, perhaps because I am neither a linguist nor a musicologist, I do not feel that the tapes we brought back are of much ethnographic significance.

While the tape recorder was, when working, a harmless toy, the movie camera and its supporting equipment (tripod, light meter, special dehumidifying containers, lenses, film) rapidly became instruments of sheer horror. Although Ruth and I knew how to use these things, neither of us were very adept at it. Setting up the tripod, taking a light reading, focusing the camera, and then trying to get someone to do something "spontaneous" for the record turned out to be a sweaty, annoying, and time-consuming process. I think it might have been worthwhile, however, if the heat had not made the metal swell so that we were never sure whether the camera was going to run or not.

The final blow came one day when I got up at 3:00 in the morning to film the yearly crop-planting ceremony. (There are some things that even the most loyal wife will not do, whatever blandishments one employs.) A group of people had agreed to take me upstream to the fields in a canoe. Now, the canoe is not an aboriginal Semai artifact, and it became obvious that this particular canoe had not been put together very skillfully when, just after we got out of sight of the settlement, it began to sink. I could not help bail it out, because I felt I had to keep all the movie equipment dry, even though it meant letting my notebook get soaked. To safeguard the equipment, then, I sat with the camera held high in one hand, the light meter in the other, the tripod balanced precariously on my knees and the icy waters of the Telom River gradually rising over my groin up to my waist, at which point we decided to beach the canoe and dump out the water. The rest of the trip to the fields went in short spurts of frenetic paddling, bailing, and trying to find places to beach the canoe in order to get the water out of it. By the time we had inched our soggy way upstream to the fields, the sun was up, and the day was getting very hot, although the water remained icy.

We landed in a swamp, in front of a vast barrier of fallen tree trunks and thorny brush left over from clearing the fields. Normally the Semai get over this sort of obstacle by running along the trunks of the topmost trees. Normally I got over them by clutching the trunks with hands and knees and hunching myself along inchworm style to the accompaniment of merry Semai laughter. A fall can be a very serious matter in Malaya, since so many plants have poisonous spines or bristles that a basic rule in falling is not to try to grab hold of anything. Near a field, there is also the possibility of falling on a piece of split bamboo, the edges of which are razor sharp. In fact, Williams-Hunt, the only person to work extensively with the Semai before we did, died as the result of such a fall. By the time I had managed to extricate myself and the movie equipment from the canoe, however, there was only one person left within hailing range, and it was clear that I would have to carry most of the things myself. The man nearby agreed to take the tripod, and, clutching the tree trunks with one hand, the movie camera with the other, the still camera slung around my neck, and the light meter between my teeth (my pockets were still too wet to store it there), I hunched slowly along to the fields. By the time I got there, of course, the ceremony was over. I was dripping with sweat and feeling like the Ancient Mariner on a bad day. Nevertheless, I decided to film the planting itself. Getting the tripod set up on the glass-slick, wet, 45-degree slopes of the field under a blazing sun was rather hard, but eventually I managed it. I took a light reading on the meter, got the scene in focus, pushed the button to start the camera and was rewarded with a single click. The thing was not running. Trying to shield the film from the sun with my none too ample body, I opened the camera, checked the wheels to make sure the film was wound correctly, pushed the button, and got a gratifying whirr as the wheels spun around. I closed the camera case, took another light reading, got the lens refocused, pushed the button, and got another single click. I repeated the whole process another couple of times, and then my temper blew. I addressed several well-chosen phrases in English to the camera, went on to a general diatribe about taking movies in the field, and concluded with a series of totally unjustifiable remarks about the American Museum of Natural History, which had been generous enough to lend us the camera in the first place. Fortunately, none of the Semai could understand what I was saying. Since I had been unable to keep the notebook from being soaked on the trip, all I could do was shoot a few still photographs of the planting. Normally I would have stayed to help out, but I was too tired physically and emotionally to think of anything but going home to bed. I managed to get back afoot largely by composing mental letters to the American Museum. I arrived with what turned out to be the incipient stages of acute pneumonitis and a firm resolve to send the movie equipment back on the next boat to come upriver with our supplies. In short, while I think movies can be of immense ethnographic value, there are situations in which they are not worth the effort required.

The rest of the recording equipment, however, was well worth taking. The still photographs illustrate many aspects of Semai life that would be very hard to describe in words. We kept one set for our own reference and gave another to the American Museum of Natural History, where copies are available to anyone interested enough to write for them.

We also used several sets of forms, including a few we made up in the field. From the point of view of our theoretical interests, the most important was the one on plants and animals. Most of the material we gathered remains to be published, but the reader can get some idea of the sort of information we collected by looking at three minor articles of mine (Dentan 1967, 1968a, 1968e). For material culture, we followed the format used by Osgood (1940), although we were able to be somewhat more detailed, since Semai society is still functioning, whereas Osgood's Ingalik society was not. The data we collected in this way are on file at the American Museum of Natural History and, people there say, constitute one of the most extensive, if not the most extensive, documentations of any collections they have.

For information about household composition and relationships between households, vital to an understanding of social organization, we asked the standard anthropological questions (for which, see, for example, Appell 1969). We also worked out in the field a schedule for inventorying household possessions. Unfortunately, much of our data on household composition, genealogy, and life histories were lost when our canoe tipped over during a tricky portage over a fallen log on our last trip downstream from the first settlement. Before we moved into the second settlement, Ruth Lim of the Malayan Institute for Medical Research supplied us with a modified version of a World Health Organization form which is used by investigators all over the world (for this form, see Thomson 1960: 36–42). We found this a better research tool than the ones we had been using, since it applied not only to household composition and possessions but to economics, health, and nutrition as well. Although there are several reasons it might not have been as useful in the first settlement, I regret not having known about it before.

We also took along a copy of the *Outline of Cultural Materials* (Murdock *et al.* 1961). This book lists the sorts of information an ethnography should contain and spurred us to collect data we might otherwise have ignored. It is also divided into convenient numbered categories that we used to label the cards on which we typed up our field notes every evening. Using this system makes it much easier, after one gets home, to find specific data one has collected, although I confess that despite an elaborate set of cross references, I sometimes have had the maddening experience of being unable to dig out information that I know is in the files. The bitter irony of the loss of our household census and genealogy notebook was that we thought it so well organized that there was no need to type it up. We did not make this error in the second settlement.

Finally, Ruth worked out a questionnaire that got at the problem of the age at which children acquired specific skills. Again, it would have been advantageous to have used this questionnaire in the first settlement, but, as Ruth freely admits, she did not really get the hang of "scientific" fieldwork until we got to the second settlement.

There are three reasons we used all these forms, the administering of which was often boring to us, the Semai, or to everyone involved. The first is that we wanted to be as systematic as possible in collecting data, in order to avoid finding embarrassing gaps in our information when we returned. I have found, and been frustrated by, several such gaps in data we gathered in more haphazard ways. The second reason was that we wanted to do statistical analyses of the data we gathered this way, in order to see whether patterns emerged of which we, and perhaps the Semai themselves, were unaware. Finally, most of these forms are constructed in such a way that the information on them can readily be translated into code numbers and punched onto IBM cards for computer analysis. So far we have cards only for plants and animals, but eventually I hope to get as much of our information encoded this way as possible.

We decided to buy as much of our living equipment in Malaya as possible, in order to seem as little "exotic" as we could. We therefore were able to arrive with one trunk and a gargantuan shoulder bag in which we kept all our essential papers and the like and which Ruth had to lug around whenever we were in town. The only "exotic" living equipment we brought into the field comprised a mattress, a flashlight, a kerosene stove, medicines, a pressure lantern, and a water filter. Of these things, the most satisfactory was the ordinary, cotton-filled mattress we used in the first settlement. In a moment of misguided inspiration, I decided that we would use inflatable rubber mattresses in the second settlement. After about a week, both began to leak, so that going to bed required inflating the mattresses, flinging ourselves on them immediately, and trying to get to sleep before they went completely flat.

Although the medicines probably kept us alive, they were, like the shots we took before going into the field, less than absolutely effective. For instance, we took prophylactic doses of chloroquine to keep from getting malaria—a disease which, incidentally, could have been wiped out several years before if the World Health Organization had been able to muster the necessary funds. Thanks partly to the Vietnam war, however, chloroquine-resistant strains of malaria have evolved, and Ruth contracted so-called "benign" tertian malaria. Her sickness not only brought us out of the field for a while, but also, when she had a relapse in New York City, we had to spend several days convincing her doctor that a New Yorker could really have malaria. Similarly, my typhoid and paratyphoid shots proved so ineffective that I found myself standing out in the rain with a typhoid-induced temperature of 106° recording a version of the ceremony that I had missed the year before because of the movie camera fiasco and felt I could not afford to miss again.

Our possession of medicines also put us into a personal dilemma involving professional goals and ordinary human decency. On the one hand, we had the resources to cure or at least alleviate the suffering that some of the people around us, many of them our friends, were undergoing. On the other hand, we were not medically trained, and there was always a possibility that the people we gave medicine to might die anyway. Just by giving out medicines, we were running the risk of alienating the local Semai curers. In the case of a death, moreover, we feared that people might hold us responsible because we had given the patient an "exotic" medicine. That kind of community response would, of course, completely ruin our rapport with the Semai and thus destroy the possibility of doing good fieldwork.

Fortunately, Semai curers are usually willing to try out anything that might benefit their patients (compare Bolton 1968:818–819 for a description of the readiness of Semai curers to complement their own techniques and medicines with Western medicines). In the first settlement, I was able to work out a deal with a prominent curer, whereby he would use our medicines in addition to his own curative techniques. So successful was this arrangement that, when I once complimented him on his skill in curing, he felt the success of this cure was due to the combination of his skills with my medicines. In the second settlement, however, I stupidly forgot to make this kind of arrangement. When the child of a close friend of mine there became very sick, I panicked and urged my friend to take the baby to a Euro-American-style clinic that was fairly nearby. The local Semai curer was miffed, quite understandably, since from his point of view I was completely unqualified to intervene in the course of treatment he had already prescribed. He therefore forbade taking the baby to the clinic on the grounds that mixing medicines would make it yet more sick. The baby died, and then two more infants sickened and died of the same ailment, without my being able to do anything. Finally, the curer's own grandchild began to develop the same symptoms, and, feeling that his previously proven techniques were no longer effective, he came to me to talk about alternatives. We agreed to try the clinic, supplemented by his own curative methods. The child lived. The point is that, by my ethnocentric failing to treat as a professional a man who was, in his own terms, a professional, I am partly responsible for the death of three human beings.

Except for the flashlight, the rest of the "exotic" living equipment we brought into the field was superfluous. Ruth soon found it easier to cook on a Semai hearth than on the kerosene stove, which we gave away quite early. I was always afraid of the pressure lantern in our extremely inflammable bamboo and thatch house. For a while, I pumped it up in front of the house, attracting a large group of giggling Semai onlookers. After a few weeks, this procedure made me feel so ridiculous that I gave the lantern away too, and we used the usual Semai kerosene "candles."

Finally, we used the water filter for the same reason that we did not eat fresh vegetables and did both boil and chlorinate our water. That is, we did not want to get sick. Given that we did want to do participant observation and that, perhaps naively, we chose two very unhealthy areas to work in, the goal of staying healthy was unrealistic. We had to eat out with other people like everyone else, especially since we wanted to observe eating rituals and to collect the nutritional data that were subsequently analyzed for us by the Institute for Medical Research. For all our contention that we were so susceptible to "water spirits" that we could only drink the tea we brought with us, boiled, it is impossible for the Semai to keep their hands so antiseptic that they do not transmit disease when they hand one food. Furthermore, both the areas we lived in were so hot that, simply to cool off, we had to go sit in the river several times a day. The rivers of Malaya carry a fantastic set of nasty microorganisms. So, despite the filter, I managed to get a bad case of infectious hepatitis, which again forced us out of the field. The only people in Malaya with enough gamma globulin to prevent Ruth's catching the disease from me were the Peace Corps. After a good deal of pleading and cajolery from lower-echelon members, their high command graciously granted Ruth half the amount she needed to keep from falling sick, with the result that her stay in the hospital was shorter than mine. In fairness to the Peace Corps, I must say that their medical personnel at Kuala Lipis, the town from which we got our supplies, were far nicer to us than they had to be, although we could not help being amused by the fact that the town they regarded as a wilderness outpost was the place we came to be cured and to taste the delights of civilization.

There was one other disease we acquired as a result of participant observation, for all our water filter and chlorine tablets. (I am omitting from this account sicknesses due to my weak lungs and those that did not interfere seriously with fieldwork, like jungle rot and ordinary dysentery.) Amebiasis is a worldwide affliction (Chandler and Read 1961: 62–63), which is very hard to cure and which most anthropologists catch in the field. I was lucky enough to be one of the three out of four "sufferers" who show few symptoms until their livers start rotting, but Ruth got not only amebic dysentery but also the appendicitis that sometimes results from this disease. The appendicitis developed on the Dutch freighter we were taking back to America. While freighters provide the cheapest and most luxurious mode of travel available, they carry no doctors, and we discovered that an appendectomy would have to be performed by a totally untrained officer, in the notoriously choppy Indian Ocean, on the basis of instructions radioed from Holland. We and the crew, with the exception of the fourth mate who was to perform the operation and was looking forward to it, found this prospect frightening. Ruth and I did not have enough funds to forfeit our passage money, however, and we all spent several tense hours before the shipping company's agent agreed to grant us passage on another vessel so that Ruth could have her appendectomy in a hospital ashore.

Under the circumstances, it is unsurprising that much as she prepares for sleep in America by reading a few chapters in a murder mystery, Ruth used to spend the hour before bed in the field reading the *Merck Manual of Diagnosis and Therapy* (Lyght 1956) to see what diseases we might have contracted that day, although her diagnoses were almost always wildly astray. It is also not surprising that she contends she would not have gone into the field if she had known the sort of physical and psychological traumas that would befall her. And, finally, I think it says something about the nature of our fieldwork that she also asserts that she wants to go back.

MEETING THE SEMAI

After arriving in Singapore, a city with which we immediately fell in love, we contacted Dr. Burkill of the Singapore Botanic Gardens, who generously agreed to lend us plant presses and the services of a trained Malay plant collector so that we could get the plants the local people used identified and preserved. We spent the next couple of weeks visiting various groups of Malayan aborigines, with the guidance of Dr. Ivan Polunin of the University of Singapore; Dr. I. Y. Carey, head of the Department of Aborigines; Inche' Ruslan, then Protector of Aborigines in the State of Johore; and Inche' Badrillah, Protector of Aborigines in the State of Pahang. Most of the groups we visited seemed very acculturated. We were tempted to work with the Jah Hut, because of their warm hospitality and stated desire to have their way of life recorded. We did visit the Jah Hut when we were in Pahang recuperating from one of the diseases that occasionally brought us out of the field. We collected some ethnographic data and a few artifacts for the American Museum of Natural History. Nevertheless, when we left the Jah Hut for the last time, one man said accurately, though in a kind way, "You will come back. You have the skin of our way of life, but you do not have the meat."

Finally, Inche' Badrillah arranged for us to go up the Telom River to visit a relatively unacculturated group, the Semai. For the first time we had a close look at virgin tropical rain forest. Like an Arctic landscape, the forest has a beauty that is utterly inhuman. But, whereas the Arctic's inhumanity lies in the near absence of life, the forest's is due to the lush abundance of all sorts of life, each of which seems to be competing with all the rest for limited resources of sun, food, and survival. I was to come to feel that the primal forest was the "real world" in a way that tamed landscapes could never be. Wallace Stevens comes close to describing this sort of feeling in a poem called *Arrival at the Waldorf*, when he describes how, after seeing a Guatemalan rain forest, he finds life in New York both more human and more superficial, "After that alien, point-blank, green and actual Guatemala." [1] Probably my love-hate feeling about the forest was intensified by the fact that I came down with a severe bronchial disease after each of three day-long trips through it.

There were two reasons for picking the particular settlement of Semai we eventually chose, although it was in some ways atypical. First, it was right on the banks of the river, only a couple of hours' raft trip from a "jungle fort," a government outpost with a radio that we could use to summon help in an emergency. The feeling of security this gave us turned out to be somewhat illusory, since, like most mechanical equipment in a tropical rain forest, the radio was not always in working condition and since, when we did get through to Kuala Lipis, that town's limited number of motor canoes were usually out up some river other than the Telom. The result was that, when we fell seriously sick, we often had to wait about a week, gobbling antibiotics and trying to do ethnography, before the canoe came to take us to the hospital. The second reason for picking this settlement was that it was relatively large and just across the river from another settlement. This situation allowed us to observe and talk with a fair-sized number of people, thus lessening the chance that the information we collected would reflect the bias of individuals or small groups rather than general Semai opinion.

Inche' Ahmat, the government official who came with us, explained to the Semai that we wanted to live for a while in their settlement. He also tried, and failed, to explain what we were trying to do. After we had moved in, I also tried many times to explain what we were up to: "We're trying to write a book about your way of life so that people in America and your own children and grandchildren will know how you lived." For people most of whom had never seen a book, none of whom was literate, none of whom had ever heard of America (to the end, they were convinced we were British), and none of whom could see any reason for outsiders to be interested in how they lived, this explanation was not merely incomprehensible but also obviously some sort of cover story. I finally settled on: "We're writing a report for the government about

---

[1] From *Collected Poems of Wallace Stevens*. Copyright 1942 by Wallace Stevens. By permission of Alfred A. Knopf, Inc.

what you eat, to see if you have enough food." The second explanation was accepted, but it led to the tacit inference that we were government officials living on government supplies. When, after about six months, I caught on to this assumption and explained that we had to buy our supplies with our own money, people were quite surprised and moderated their demands for food and tobacco.

At any rate, Inche' Ahmat and the people picked out a small "deserted" house in which we could live. We promised to be back in a few days, after getting our supplies. The owner of the house returned a few months later but, despite our offers to move out, he went next door to live with some relatives. Fortunately, the Semai feel that there is a special affinity between people who have slept in the same sleeping place and thus breathed the fragrance of each other's bodies. The result of this feeling was that the owner and I quickly became good friends.

We made two major mistakes in this process of choosing and gaining entrée into this settlement. We avoided them when we went to the second settlement. First we picked the second settlement in an area where medical assistance was relatively easy to get. On the other hand, we also ignorantly picked the hottest and most humid area in hot, humid Malaya. Second, instead of having Malays bring us in, Dr. Bolton, the devoted head of the medical branch of the Department of Aborigines, kindly asked some of his Semai medical aides to introduce us to a settlement where they had relatives. At the first settlement, we did not initially realize the intensity of the suspicion the Semai feel toward Malays. Although both Inche' Ahmat and our plant collector were consistently polite and friendly to the Semai, their very presence with us made us suspicious characters. After a couple of weeks I realized this association was making rapport difficult. I had to send the Malay plant collector downstream and train a Semai one.

In the second settlement, we had the same pleasant experience with a "deserted" house that we had in the first. My pat "government report on food" explanation, however, fell flat. The man who was to become our adoptive father said that such a report might be useful. Nevertheless, he went on, what he would really like to see was a book about the Semai way of life, so that Americans and his own people's children and grandchildren would know how the Semai lived.

Living in the First Settlement ("East Semai")

THE FIRST DAY

When we returned with our supplies to the first settlement, we found that the people had added a porch to our house. They had also taken a hibiscus shrub from the jungle fort and planted it in front of the house, because, when they were interned during the communist uprising of the early 1950s, they had

The men have just finished covering a grave with banana leaves and are starting to build a shelter over it (1962).

A seven-year-old East Semai girl with a cigar (1962).

East Semai boy playing nose flute (1962).

noticed that "pale people" camp commandants seemed to like flowers growing around their houses.

Although people were wary of me at first, their wariness was based on the fact that I was at least partially a known quantity: a "pale person," a *Tuan* (a respectful Malay title used for Englishmen), presumably somewhat like the British officers they had encountered during the communist insurgency. Most people in the first settlement called me Tuan throughout our stay, although a few good friends gave me affectionate or joking nicknames. Ruth, however, was another matter. No one I talked to about the matter had ever seen a female "pale person" before. A few people addressed her, hesitantly, as Tuan, but they seemed to feel, correctly, that the term did not properly apply to a woman. Ruth finally broke the ice by announcing in her faltering Malay that she wanted to learn to live like a Semai woman. A swarm of giggling and chattering women immediately gathered around her, swept her up the ladder into our house, stripped her naked, wrapped her in a sarong, stuck flowers into her hair, painted her face, put a machete into her hand, and took her off to collect firewood. She quickly became *Ua' Roi*. *Ua'* is the term for a young woman (compare our "Miss"), and *Roi*, the closest the Semai could come to pronouncing "Ruth," means "housefly."

Another large group of people were examining me, much as if I were a particularly bizarre museum specimen. Only four people did much talking to me. The titular headman, who was acting in his official capacity as group spokesman, was an old, cynical, shrewd, and manipulative man, at the time of our arrival primarily interested in what benefits our stay might bring him personally. He was a Semai-ized Temiar, and my impression is that the Temiar, at least in that settlement, are less timid and more greedy than the Semai. I never got to know him very well, partly because he became tired of living on the Telom and went back to the Jelai river basin, where he felt he belonged. Another Semai-ized Temiar, Rambutan, a grey-haired elderly man from across the river, was also friendly to me, but his remarks indicated that he also, albeit in a subtle way, was mainly interested in what he could get out of us. He later became one of my main informants but so delighted in putting me on that I feel I can rely on his information only when I have corroborative data from other sources. I doubt, for example, that he ever saw the baby dragons (*naga'*) whose habits he detailed from his "personal observations." Ours was to be a purely working relationship, modified by a little mutual kidding. The third man to do much talking was a prematurely balding local curer named, appropriately, Uproar. He was far more overtly opportunistic than the two Temiar. We later came to know and like each other well, and he was one of my best and most articulate informants. Our relationship remained on a joking level, however, and there was never any question that in his interaction with me, as in his dealings with other Semai, the thought uppermost in Uproar's mind was usually "What's in it for me?" I was later to develop a much warmer relationship with his much shyer and less-well-informed younger brother, a man about my age and almost as neurotic and intense as I am. The only other person to do much conversing was Stump, a sturdy man in his thirties, with a hot temper, a difficult personal characteristic for a Semai to live with. He and his wife, a woman who always wanted to gossip about sex with Ruth, became our best friends in the settlement. When Stump and Rambutan became involved in a dispute about whether Rambutan was responsible for the haunting of Stump's house by the ghosts of people Rambutan had buried, Stump moved out of the settlement, and Ruth and I used to trek the half hour or so upstream to Stump's new house just to chat, about once a week. (Of course, as I pointed out above, anthropologists rarely just chat. There is always in each chat information to be recorded.)

On the first day, naturally, no one emerged as a personality. We felt in a sea of undifferentiated, small, honey-colored people, who would sometimes help us by carrying and arranging things, sometimes hinder us by their sheer numbers as they packed into our tiny house. The crowd with me blended with the crowd that followed Ruth when she emerged, exhausted, hands covered with blisters, from the forest. No one left the house when Ruth suggested that she wanted to lie down and take a nap. There were still masses of bodies in the house when we wanted to cook supper. We knew we could not feed them all, we did not know that the Semai do not think it imperative to feed guests when one does not have enough food, and so we settled down grimly to outwait them before cooking. By 11 P.M. most of the people had gone home. Ruth prepared a meal for us, and the remaining half-dozen visitors ate gustily while making disparaging remarks about the caliber of Ruth's cooking. After they left, we collapsed into bed, only to notice that inside our mosquito net were small, moving streaks of light. A check with the flashlight revealed that the lights were luminous centipedes. Ruth insisted on a thorough check of bed and mosquito net, an exploration that uncovered a variety of small, unpleasant fauna. By the time we got to sleep that first night, we were well into culture shock and resolved to check the bed nightly.

Problems in Doing Fieldwork

PRIVACY

My purpose in sketching some of the personalities and relationships that eventually emerged from the undifferentiated mass of humanity we met the first day is to introduce two problems we encountered in the field: (1) the difficulty of getting any privacy without disrupting the good relationships upon which our anthropological work and emotional well being depended, and (2) the disruptive effect of having outsiders come to visit us. The notion of privacy is rather alien to the Semai, except insofar as people of opposite sexes are not supposed to spy in order to see each other's naked genitals. For us to tell a man with whom we had a good relationship that we did not want to see him at a certain time, simply because we wanted to be alone, would have been a gross, incomprehensible insult. He would have been put in a state of ritual danger, and, if he did not feel that we had terminated our relationship with him, he would almost certainly have broken it off himself. On the other hand, as bourgeois Americans, we were used to houses with thick-walled rooms that insulate an individual or couple from others, so that the inhabitants can be alone to think, read, write, or perform "intimate" biological activities. We found it inhibiting, for example, when trying to indulge in a little connubial bliss in our creaky house, when Uproar, our next door neighbor, would shout jokingly, "Hey, what are you two doing in there?"

Similarly, I found it hard to adapt to the fact that going to the river to defecate meant answering cries of "Where are you going?" The evasive answer, "To the river," merely led people to ask, "Why are you going to the river?" A mumbled "To defecate" brought a reply of either "Have a good defecation" or, sometimes, if the speaker was a man, "Hang on, I'll come with you." To reject his proffered companionship would have risked ruining our relationship.

Sometimes I could sneak off, but, since Semai women tend to be even more gregarious than the men, Ruth almost always had a few companions. As she once remarked, "We squat there in a row in the water, with our sarongs up, like a bunch of ducks." The day Ruth discovered the value of this gregariousness came when she managed to slip off alone and found on her way back a tiger between herself and the settlement. She ran upstream, tried to find another path to the settlement, lost the path, and at last decided that, if she had to die, she wanted to die in the water. On her return, fortunately, the tiger had gone, leaving only a few paw marks in the sand. After that, she preferred having the women accompany her.

Although gregariousness did have its advantages, and although our thirst for privacy was in part just a bit of "pale people" ethnocentrism that we had to cast off in order to live with Semai, nevertheless the lack of privacy impeded our fieldwork in two ways. First, we were working from 5 or 6 A.M. to 11 or 12 P.M. every day at jobs that were often intellectually, emotionally, and/or physically exhausting. We needed an occasional break just to keep going. After about a month, we hit on the idea of a weekly "taboo day," on which we were "ritually unable" to do much socializing unless something unusual happened or visitors came from another settlement. The Semai, knowing of the Malay sabbath, could understand this sort of ritual restriction. Although we were never able to have a completely uninterrupted "taboo day," we were able to get in a little reading, sleeping, and letter-writing.

The other difficulty with having a house full of people all the time was that the constant chatter tended to distract informants, especially if they found the topic under discussion complicated or boring. Since most of the adults spent at least part of the day working, children were the main problem. My solution was to give each child a pen and some file cards, asking him to draw pictures of people, houses, and trees. When the child was leaving, I collected the drawings; noted the artist's name, sex, and age; and later filed the pictures. Drawings of this kind correspond with the sort of material elicited by a certain psychological test. I distrust the reliability of such tests, especially when used cross-culturally and in this sort of haphazard way. Nevertheless, it is interesting that (1) the drawings are very much like those made by Black American children, presumably because both groups feel outside the dominant culture and (2) two psychiatrists, neither of whom had any previous knowledge of the Semai, independently induced from these drawings an idea of Semai personality that tends strongly to confirm my own ideas.

I regret not also having had both children and adults draw pictures of food organisms, since such drawings might have revealed what features of the organism they found most striking. These features in turn might have served as useful clues as to how the Semai classify organisms and why certain rituals focus on certain organisms. One reason this omission is so frustrating is that I failed to take advantage of several other chances to discover such distinguishing features. For instance, I could not get specimens of all the things the Semai eat. Hence I could not rely entirely on the good offices of the Singapore Botanic Gardens or the Zoology Department at the then University of Malaya for identifications. I therefore tried to get informants to give the Semai words for some organisms of which I had drawings or pictures. Although I tried to check this information by also getting the Malay name, usually the Semai did not know the Malay word. In most cases, informants also disagreed about the Semai name for the organism depicted. The intelligent thing would have been to take a group of Semai to the Singapore Botanic Gardens and to the zoological collection at the University of Malaya.

If I had not been so obsessed with identifying the organisms, however, I would have realized that there were at least three research possibilities opened up by this difficulty in getting Semai names for the organisms in the pictures. First, there may be real disagreements about the names for plants and animals of certain kinds. Unquestionably, people in different settlements often do use different terms for the same species (Dentan 1967b), a fact that may have something to do with Semai ecology and social structure (Gardner 1966). Some of the apparent Semai confusion, however, may have really been mine. Different people may have been giving me words that referred to categories of different levels of generality, as an American might call a certain animal a "dog" or a "spaniel" (Frake 1961). Although what I do know about Semai taxonomy makes me think this possibility unlikely in most cases, not investigating it was a mistake. The most interesting possibility, however, in terms of finding out what features of the organism the Semai find striking, is that different people responded to different features of the picture. All I had to ask was "What makes you think this is a picture of that?" None of these ideas occurred to me in the field.

VISITORS

Given the Semai attitude toward outsiders, non-Semai visitors posed a threat to our relationships with Semai. In both settlements we had to be somewhat standoffish toward Malays who came to meet us. The Semai helped us maintain this rather ungracious attitude by, for example, whispering in Semai slang, "Don't take the cigarette that Malay's offering you. It's probably poisoned." Since most of the "pale people" who came to visit us were those too insensitive to pick up our obvious reluctance to have visitors who as "pale people" were so clearly identified with us, we used to have to spend much of the time they were around explaining to the Semai why they acted so rudely. For us, although the incident did not disrupt our relationship with any Semai, the most upsetting visit was that of a buxom, young, female "pale person" about 5 feet 10 inches tall. We decided, rather maliciously, to maximize her exposure to the Semai by getting her a sleeping compartment in a longhouse. Unluckily, the compartment she got was that of Bah Chong, an adolescent boy about whom we felt very fond and protective, partly because he was an orphan and no woman in the settlement would sleep with him, since he was short (4 feet 6 inches), very dark skinned, and had a goiter so large that it tilted his sensitive face slightly to one side. I was unaware, at that time, of the Semai equation between sleeping place, body fragrance, and personal affinity. The upshot was that, while the other men in the settlement were making snide comments like, "Wah, she's big! *Ua' Roi* (Ruth) is fine, but this one's too much," Chong fell deeply in love with our visitor. For the rest of our stay, Chong was always talking about her, dreaming of her, and coming to our house to sleep because he could not face the day without her. She, of course, had gone off after a week with no idea of the emotional disaster she had created. My own feeling is that I will never visit any anthropologist in the field, and I hope that no one will visit me.

SOME PROBLEMS THAT DID NOT ARISE

One factor that we had feared might disrupt our relationships with the community was the fact that, to get the exhaustive data on food and ritual we wanted, we knew that we would have to disrupt the local economy and perhaps seem to be playing favorites. For example, we wanted to observe what people ate, since direct observation is more reliable than the "recall method" used in the WHO form.[2] In order not to bias our data, we could neither give nor accept

---

[2] In such tests informants are asked to recall what they had eaten over a given period of time.

food from members of the household under observation. Since one way the Semai demonstrate mutual good will is by exchanging food, we feared we might lose rapport with the people we were observing. Perhaps because we picked people with whom we already had good relationships and because we promised a bonus of food at the end of the two-week observational period, the people we worked with cooperated without losing any rapport.

A similar but potentially more serious problem was posed by the fact that we had to pay some people to do boring things like collecting specimens, making artifacts, and answering repetitive form questions about the specimens and artifacts. Fortunately, the Semai were as worried about their personal relationships as we were about ours. In both communities, our paid informants asked that we keep the fact that we were paying them a secret. We were delighted to do so, since knowledge of such payment again might have made people think we were playing favorites. I think most people in both settlements suspected that we were paying certain informants. The reason for this suspicion was not only that informants spent a lot more time with us and did more things for us than other people did, but also that the informants themselves were so caught up in the traditional economy that they eventually gave away many of the things we secretly bought for them out of their wages. The habit of giving was too hard to break. Nevertheless, almost everyone was willing to turn a blind eye to such facts, presumably because they did not want to upset their relationships with the paid informants and with us.

A PROBLEM THAT TURNED OUT TO BE HELPFUL

The list of personal and methodological difficulties we met could be indefinitely expanded. Given our positive feelings about our field experience, however, it seems fitting to conclude this section by describing an apparent problem that eventually helped us understand our data better. For each food the Semai ate I tried to find out, among other things, whether people should eat it during pregnancy, just after having a child, while menstruating, before reaching a certain age, and so forth. I also tried to find out why people thought they should refrain from eating these foods. Uproar, our first paid informant, gave what seemed to be dogmatic and unequivocal answers to these questions. Casual chatting with other people, however, revealed that, although they largely agreed with Uproar about which foods should be avoided at what times, they gave entirely different reasons for the avoidances. I then systematically spot-checked with other Semai about one in every dozen of the 500 odd foods Uproar and I had listed. I found the same pattern of fairly good agreement about the avoidances and the same disagreement about reasons. I used a wide variety of informants and did not say that I was trying to check up on Uproar's reliability, lest personal factors influence people's answers.

The results of this spot-check disturbed me, because I thought Uproar and I were good enough friends that he would not consistently mislead me. There was also a methodological problem. Most Semai dislike openly disagreeing with each other or being caught out in inconsistencies. I therefore could not confront Uproar directly with explanations that ran counter to his own. If the dissenter were absent, I knew Uproar would say, as he had about disagreements in the past, "Oh, him. He's a liar." If the dissenter were present, I would run the risk of precipitating a quarrel, which would make life in the settlement harder for everyone, including Ruth and myself. And I had already had the experience, when I asked someone to repeat information that he knew I had written down, of being told "Read back to me what I said, and I'll tell you whether you've got it right," with the clear implication that the informant was not about to risk contradicting what he had already said. How, then, was I to determine Uproar's reliability?

I eventually decided to rely on the sheer bulk of the material. Uproar could not be expected to remember whether he had already answered questions about a minor food item on the list. I therefore acted as if every new specimen some-one brought us was one we had never discussed, whether or not we had. Uproar's answers were fairly consistent about the avoidances but totally inconsistent about the rationales. I next went over the entire list with Rambutan and then with Uproar's younger brother. Again, I found that they tended to agree with Uproar about the avoidances but disagreed with Uproar, other informants, each other, and (under the "forgetfulness test") themselves about why one should avoid a certain food at certain times. The crowning touch came when, eating with Uproar's younger brother, I noticed his pregnant wife eating rat, which he had just told me pregnant women should not eat. To my question, he replied, "That's right, I keep asking her not to, but she just doesn't care." Further investigation revealed that many people who had never had any problems during, say, preg-nancy, tended to eat the foods they were supposed to avoid.

The point I want to make is that the very inconsistency of these facts is informative. First, it suggests that explanations for these food rituals may rest on idiosyncratic personal experience. I was able to find several cases in which specific individuals avoided certain foods on certain occasions because they had had something bad happen to them after eating those foods on a similar occasion. The personalism of these explanations fits in neatly with the appar-ently personalistic inconsistencies in naming animals. Second, people's responses indicated that they followed the rituals only when they felt in danger. In other words, the greater the anxiety, the greater the likelihood that the ritual will be performed—a point long debated in anthropology. Finally, the inconsistency of the rationales for the rituals suggest that the ritual is the important and prior thing, the explanation merely a subsequent rationalization of the ritual. If the Semai had codified these explanations, I might have been deluded into thinking that the explanations were supernatural sanctions for avoiding foods. Again, although the idea that ritual precedes belief is an old one (dating back at least to 1889; Robertson Smith 1956:21), anthropologists still argue about it. In short, the very incoherence of the Semai data, which really bothered me in the field, actually sheds some light on current anthropological interests.

Living in the Second Settlement ("West Semai")

INTRODUCTION

There are three reasons this section is shorter than the one on the first settlement. (1) We were faced with far fewer problems of adaptation to the people. We spoke Semai, albeit with an odd East Semai-American accent. We knew how to act Semai. Conversely, the Semai in the second settlement were more used to the oddities of "pale people," and because we had been introduced by Semai, they were more willing to accept us. (2) Logistically, we were much better off. For example, in the first settlement, our supplies came upriver once a month. For a while each month, therefore, we seemed to the people, who got their own food in small daily amounts, to be selfishly hoarding a huge surplus. In the west we could buy our food in small daily amounts at the local market, as many of the Semai themselves did. Moreover, since the traditional exchange system was breaking down, people made fewer demands on our supplies. Another advantage was that travel was so much easier that we could visit distant settlements where Semai friends had relatives. Such visits provided us with interesting comparative data. Finally, we were physically much more comfortable. (3) Most of the personal and methodological problems we faced were so much like those we faced in the east that we were able to counter them with solutions we had already worked out.

PERSONAL RELATIONSHIPS

Because mutual adaptation was easier, we were able to form personal relationships much more quickly than in the east. In general these relationships were much warmer and less beset by mutual misunderstanding. I still correspond occasionally with my adoptive father and with Daylight, my principle informant and a real intellectual. (An anthropologist currently at work in the same settlement writes that Daylight is so reliable that he tends to take Daylight's word over the statements of people actually involved in an incident.) I had hoped to dig out these letters for information, but they almost all follow this form:

No news here, only good news. Send a photograph of yourselves and your house. We miss you. When are you coming back? We wish you the best of everything.

Sometimes the writer will mention a death or a marriage, and once Daylight asked me to help finance his niece's wedding feast. Most of the time, however, our Semai correspondents seem to feel that letters are to transmit not information but affection.

One sign of the ease with which we slipped into the new community was the names people gave us. Names, for rather complex reasons, are very important to the Semai. I never had to fight the *Tuan* role but was at once *Bah Rab*. When people found out that we were both first-born children, they began sometimes calling us *Long*, that is, "first Born," with none of the East Semai hesitancy. People would also occasionally call Ruth "sterile," a nonpejorative name for a childless married woman who has been of child-bearing age for several years. Finally, when our father adopted us, I became *Bah* "obtain," since, he said, information flowed to me, "like rivers into the ocean, which is deep but never filled." Ruth became *Ua'* "success," because, "whatever she tries to do, she will succeed." Furthermore, as this instance indicates, we never had to prod the West Semai into forming fictive kin relationships with us, as we had had to prod the East Semai.

In short, although our stay in the east was more adventurous and exciting, our stay in the west was easier and more personally satisfying, with the result that our work went more smoothly and productively.

Conclusion

After leaving the second Semai settlement, we spent a month in Kuala Lumpur, the delightful capital of Malaya. With the gracious permission of the Department of Aborigines, we examined census records for all Semailand in order to find out the age and sex distribution of the population, household size, the times at which fields were cleared in various areas, the acreages cleared by specific bands, and so forth. I began writing up our data on the way back to America. Nevertheless, I do not feel that we have enough material on these complex and diverse people for me to be ready to write a full-scale ethnography. For this reason alone, I want to go back. But as should be clear by now, I also want to go back because I feel for the Semai and their country the bittersweet blend of nostalgia and homesickness that the Semai call *rəniag*.

References

Appell, G. N., 1969, Social anthropological census for cognatic societies and its application among the Rungus of northern Borneo. *Bijdragen tot de taal-, Land- en Volkenkunde* 125:80–93.

Bolton, J. M., 1968, Medical services to the aborigines in West Malaysia. *British Medical Journal* 2:818–823.

Chandler, A. C., and *C. P. Read,* 1961, *Introduction to Parasitology.* 10th ed. New York: John Wiley.

Dentan, R. K., 1964, Senoi. In F. M. Lebar, G. C. Hickey, and J. K. Musgreave, eds., *Ethnic Groups of Mainland Southeast Asia.* New Haven, Conn.: Human Relations Area Files.

————, 1967a, The response to intellectual impairment among the Semai. *American Journal of Mental Deficiency* 71:764–766.

————, 1967b, The mammalian taxonomy of the Senoi Semai. *Malayan Nature Journal* 20:100–106.

————, 1968a, Notes on Semai ethnoentomology. *Malayan Nature Journal* 21:17–28.

————, 1968b, *The Semai*. New York: Holt, Rinehart and Winston, Inc.

————, 1968c, The Semai response to mental aberration. *Bijdragen tot de Taal-, Land- en Volkenkunde* 124:135–58.

————, 1968d, Some problems in determining the conservation needs of the hill peoples of South East Asia. In *Conservation in Tropical South East Asia*. International Union for Conservation of Nature and Natural Resources n.s. Publication No. 10:89–92.

————, 1968e, Notes on Semai ethnomalacology. *Malacologia* 7:135–141.

————, 1969, Prey size and food avoidance among the Semai. Paper read at the American Association for the Advancement of Science meetings, December 27 (mimeograph).

————, 1970a, Labels and rituals in Semai classification. *Ethnology* 9:16–25.

————, 1970b, Hocus pocus and extensionism in central Malaysia. *American Anthropologist* 72:358–362.

————, 1971, Some Senoi Semai planting techniques. *Economic Botany* 25:136–159.

————, 1975, If there were no Malays, who would the Semai be? In J. Nagata (ed.), Pluralism in Malaysia: Myth and reality. *Contributions to Asian Studies* 7:50–64.

————, 1976, Identity and ethnic contact: Perak, Malaysia, 1963. In T. S. Kang (ed.), Intergroup relations: Asian scenes. *Journal of Asian Affairs* 1:79–86.

Frake, C. O., 1961, The diagnosis of disease among the Subanun of Mindanao, *American Anthropologist* 63:113–132.

Gallagher, P., 1967, Games Malinowski played. *The New Republic* 156 (24): 24–26.

Gardner, P., 1967, Symmetric respect and memorate knowledge: The structure and ecology of individualistic culture. *Southwestern Journal of Anthropology* 22:389–415.

Lyght, E., Ed., 1956, *The Merck Manual of Diagnosis and Therapy*. 9th ed. Rahway, N. J.: Merck and Co.

Malinowski, B., 1935, *Coral Gardens and Their Magic*. Bloomington: Indiana University Press.

————, 1967, *A Diary in the Strict Sense of the Term*. New York: Harcourt, Brace and World.

Murdock, G. P., et. al., 1961, *Outline of Cultural Materials*. New Haven, Conn.: Human Relations Area Files.

Osgood, C., 1940, *Ingalik Material Culture*. New Haven, Conn.: Yale University Publications in Anthropology No. 22.

Robertson Smith, W., 1956, *The Religion of the Semites*. New York: Meridian. Originally published in 1889.

Thomson, F. A., 1960, Child nutrition. A survey in the Parit District of Perak Federation of Malaya. Bulletin No. 10 from the Institute for Medical Research, Federation of Malaya.

$\boxed{13}$

Afterthoughts (1978)

Introduction

AFTER FIELDWORK (the encounter between people) is over, ethnography consists of thinking back on what happened. In the dozen years since this book first appeared I have thought about the Semai a lot. Sketching how my thinking changed seems useful in showing how ethnographers work, although the necessary brevity of this chapter makes the account rather scattershot. The section titles in this chapter are questions students and anthropologists have raised about the Semai and about ethnography in recent years.

The Semai have changed, too. In 1975, the Malaysian government felt that internal security reasons prevented any long stay with the Semai by foreigners, so that my new wife, daughter, and I spent most of our time with the Hma' Mrih (Mah Meri on the map at the beginning of this book), another indigenous Austro-Asiatic speaking people. We were able, however, to talk to Semai who were working in Kuala Lumpur, Malaysia's capital city, and to spend three weeks on a social visit with my adopted family in the west Semai settlement.

Are the Semai Really That Nice?

Many Americans felt that this book romanticized the Semai, making them seem more pleasant to be with than people could be. "Retrospective falsification" can be part of the aforementioned process of thinking back, remembering the good times and forgetting the bad. This possibility intimidated me so much that I took two months in Malaysia to work up the courage to find myself, airplane bag in hand, inching across the iron beam that was all that remained of the bridge leading to the west Semai settlement. It was like trying to cross an east Semai bamboo pole bridge. A gaggle of unrecognizable Semai children and a few adults gathered to watch my inchworm's crawl: "Look at the Pale Person trying to cross the water!"

The airplane bag proved too much of a handicap, and I retreated to a place where I could cross the gully on foot. By the time I reached the settlement the adults had decided: "You're Bah Rab of the old days, aren't you?" I was.

Two American anthropological families, the Fixes and Robarcheks,[1] had lived in the settlement since 1963, and their Semai friends had picked up some American ways of acting. Instead of traditional Semai reserve (a man may scarcely speak to a beloved brother he meets for the first time in years), I was met with hugs, weeping, and laughter. It was more like coming home than homecoming in America has ever been for me. Next day I returned to Kuala Lumpur and brought my six-year-old daughter back to my adopted parents' house. My "younger brother's" son, my namesake and "grandchild" and her "older brother," took her under his wing, although she was larger than he was. It was the first time I knew there was a child named after me. Next week my wife joined us, and we spent a couple of weeks eating, drinking, and catching up on news. In implicit tribute to the Fixes and Robarcheks several people remarked, "We get a kick out of having you Pale People around." As all the Americans involved testify, the feeling is mutual.

Are the Semai Nonviolent?

Semai children now play at karate and gunfighting, following the example set by movies. But this book uses the term "nonviolent" to mean "not doing each other physical hurt," and that they rarely, if ever, do. Official records show one murder by a Semai between 1963 and 1976. The victim was a non-Semai shopkeeper who had seduced the killer's wife and cheated him to boot, circumstances which this book indicates could lead to violence.

The "Semai case" has become of some importance in the argument between Euro-American conservatives, who contend that people are "innately aggressive," and liberals, who disagree. The argument seems foolish, since people define "aggression" whatever way suits their argument, and since no ethnographer except a Semai can crawl into a Semai head to see if there are any "aggressive impulses" there. For Euro-Americans, "it must be like a movie." Semai are not nonviolent because they have "nonviolent personalities," whatever that means. Of course Semai *can* be violent. Bah Sten Gun, who fought on both sides during the Communist insurgency, was violent. In the traditional Semai context, however, violence is distasteful and senseless. Semai are usually too intelligent to get sucked into it. People interested in pursuing this topic should read Robarchek (1977) and Montagu (1978).

How Have the Semai Changed?

Since 1963, Malaysian anthropologists have done a lot of good work, which their Euro-American colleagues have tended to overlook. The list of readings at the

---

[1] The bibliography at the end of this chapter lists anthropologists and publications mentioned.

end of this chapter includes publications with extensive bibliographies that include Malaysian sources. As late as 1978, however, Malaysian anthropologists had done little work with the Semai, so that this section rests on sketchy and impressionistic information.

To some extent, the west Semai have moved into the broader West Malaysian economy, particularly into jobs (like driving taxis, growing commercial tapioca, or collecting rainforest products) which fit the traditional Semai pattern of working hard when one feels like it but not otherwise. A man from the interior will put on trousers, shirt, and sunglasses and work in "the marketplace," as the Semai call the non-Semai world, for a year or so. Then he returns home, puts on a loincloth, picks up a blowpipe, and goes hunting. The Semai still take paramilitary jobs, but the ambush of a jeep and the death of a Temiar family riding in it in 1975 gave many people second thoughts. In general, however, moving back and forth between "cultures" seems not to bother the Semai, although, faced with competition from other people, as in the taxi business, they tend to withdraw.

Methodism has made further inroads among the west Semai since 1963. More people drink alcohol, and, although the problem is not serious in Euro-American terms, Malaysian officials are concerned. Adolescent men (*litau*) look and act like parodies of Euro-American "hippies." They tend to shun regular jobs and to support themselves by gathering rainforest products.

Although no Semai had entered college as of 1976, there were several high school graduates. People's sophistication about "marketplace" politics seems on the rise. In 1974, Semai working for the Department of Orang Asli (formerly the Department of Aborigines) tried to start a union. The effort foundered on the traditional mistrust between the Semai and the Temiar, a mistrust deepened by the fact that, because they are better educated, the Semai have replaced the Temiar as the dominant indigenous people in the Department.

In general, the rather ethnocentric "anthropologist's nightmare" that peoples will disappear or be assimilated, as in the case of the Seneca in New York or the Bretons in France, seems exaggerated in the Semai example. A far more serious question, one that everyone should probably think about, is one that a young west Semai man posed me in 1975. "You've been around a lot," he said. "Can you tell me why, wherever there are native peoples, they are always the poorest and most oppressed?"

Recommended Reading (1978)

DAHLAN, H. M. (ed.), 1976, *The Nascent Malaysian Society*. Siri Monograf Jabatan Antropologi & Sosiologi Universiti, Kebangsaan, Malaysia, #3.
    Baharon Azhar Raffei'i, head of the Department of Orang Asli, and H. M. S. Hood contribute interesting chapters on Temuan and Semelai (see map).
DELORIA, V., JR., 1970, *Custer Died for Your Sins*. New York: Avon.
    A Lakota ("Sioux") presents the case against ethnography in a chapter ironically titled "Anthropologists and Other Friends."

DUNN, F. L., 1975, *Rainforest Collectors and Traders*. Malaysian Branch of the Royal Asiatic Society Monograph #5.

A full treatment of a topic on which this book only touches.

FIX, A., 1977, *The Demography of the Senoi Semai*. University of Michigan Museum Anthropological Paper #62.

Exemplary and essential.

MONTAGU, A. (ed.), 1978, *Learning Non-Aggression*. New York: Oxford University Press.

Dentan contributes a chapter on Semai.

ROBARCHEK, C., 1977, *Semai Nonviolence*. Ph.D. thesis at University of California at Riverside, available from University Microfilms, Ann Arbor, Michigan.

The most comprehensive treatment of the topic to date.

SOCIAL ANTHROPOLOGY SECTION, SCHOOL OF COMPARATIVE SOCIAL SCIENCES, UNIVERSITI SAINS MALAYSIA, *Provisional Research Reports*.

S. Nagata and, later, A. Walker supervised this excellent series of reports, mostly on Malaysian indigenous peoples and written by talented undergraduates on the basis of fieldwork.

Glossary

English Terms

ATAP (attap): From Malay *atap*, "roofing material, thatch." Thatch made of woven palm leaves; the Semai usually use the leaves of a stemless palm, *Eugeissona tristis.* See Chapter 2.

DEPARTMENT OF ABORIGINES: A department of the Malaysian government charged with improving the lot of the Malayan aborigines by providing medical services, advice on agricultural techniques, and so forth.

FOXTAIL MILLET: A millet (q.v.), *Setaria italica*, probably first domesticated in China. The seeds are covered with long reddish-brown bristles, giving the plant the appearance its name suggests. See Chapter 3.

JOB'S TEARS: A plant (*Coix lachryma-jobi*) related to maize; produces hard white or gray "fruits"; formerly cultivated by Senoi and some Semang to provide beads. See Chapter 3.

LONGHOUSE: A single-unit, one-floored apartment house the inhabitants of which constitute a primary group, that is, an aggregation of people each of whom interacts on a face-to-face basis with all the others oftener than with outsiders. (The stipulation that the inhabitants be a primary group is meant to exclude, for example, motels.)

MALAY: From Malay *mĕlayu*, "Malay." (1) A language in the Malayo-Polynesian language family. (2) In Malaysian law, any person who speaks Malay, follow Malay customary law, and is a Moslem.

MALAYA: From *Malay.* (1) A peninsula connected to mainland Southeast Asia by th Isthmus of Kra. (2) The western part of the Federation of Malaysia.

MALAYAN: Pertaining to Malaya and its inhabitants, both Malay and non-Malay.

MILLET: Any of several kinds of cereals which generally produce grains smaller th those of sorghum or maize. See Chapter 3.

NUCLEAR FAMILY: A man, his wife, and his children.

PITCH: The slope of a roof, expressed by the ratio of the height to the span.

RATTAN: From Malay *rotan*, "rattan." (1) A climbing palm with a vine-like stem up 200 feet long. (2) A binding made by splitting a rattan stem lengthwise into lo thin strands. See Chapter 2.

SAKAI: From Malay *sakai*, non-Moslem slave. (1) Malayan aborigines; more narrowly, Malayan aborigines who do not speak Malay; most narrowly, Senoi. The term has a derogatory connotation, for example, *mĕnyakaikan* ("to treat like a Sakai") means "to treat with arrogance and contempt." (2) In the older anthropological literature, Sakai is synonymous with Senoi, for example, Northern Sakai = Temiar, Central Sakai = Semai.

SEMANG: From Semang *sǝmag* or *sǝmɔg*, "person." (1) A group of languages closely related to Senoi. (2) One or more people whose native language is Semang and who live primarily by hunting, fishing, and gathering. Semang are often said to be "negritoes," racially different from their neighbors.

SENOI: From Semai/Temiar *sǝn'oi* or *sǝng'oi*, "person." (1) A group of languages in the Austro-Asiatic language family; distantly related to Cambodian but probably unrelated to Malay; includes Semai, Temiar, Mah Meri, Jah Hut, Siwang, Semelai, and, perhaps, the language formerly spoken by the Jakun. (2) One or more people whose native language is Senoi and who are agriculturalists.

SIBLING: Brother or sister.

TAPIOCA: An American root crop, *Manihot esculenta;* also called manioc or cassava; propagated by stem-cuttings and growing to a height of 9 feet. One of the highest yielding crops known, it requires little care. Its nutritive value is less than that of most foods, and some varieties are so poisonous that people must leave a mash of the roots in a stream for several days before the poison is washed out and the mash is fit to eat. See Chapter 3.

TEKNONYMY: Custom in which a parent takes his child's name as his own. The parent's new name is called a *teknonym.*

TEMIAR: (1) A Senoi language. (2) One or more of the approximately 8000 speakers of Temiar. Temiar country borders Semai country on the north.

WEAVERFINCH: Any of many African and Asiatic birds (family Ploceidae) that construct nests of elaborately interlaced vegetation.

YAM: Large, starchy storage root of several species in the genus *Dioscorea;* propagated by tuber or stem-cuttings. Not to be confused with the sweet potato, *Ipomoea batatas.* See Chapter 3.

Semai Terms

Note: The following translations are merely rough approximations of the meanings of the Semai words. The "real" meanings are far too complex, subtle, and elusive to be expressed in a brief translation.

Bood, sǝgad: West Semai term is from Malay *sĕgan,* "reluctant, shy". Not to feel like doing something, for any reason, for example, sickness, shyness, laziness. See Chapter 6.

Gengster: W. Semai, from U.S. "gangster". A non-Semai who for rather obscure reasons goes about frightening, injuring, and sometimes even killing innocent people.

Gu: W. Semai term. A demographic unit comprising all the Semai born and raised in a given major watershed. Semai say that the people in one such watershed have the same great-great-great-great-great-grandparents (a metaphor indicating that they are "akin" to each other). *Gu* membership is for life, even for those who eventually move out of the river basin in which they were born. There seems to be a strong tendency for men to marry women from their own *gu.* See Chapters 2 and 8.

Gunig: (1) A *ruai* (more rarely, a *kǝloog*) that, under the proper circumstances, will aid a *halaa'* in the diagnosis and treatment of disease. (2) An organism with a *ruai* of this sort. See Chapter 9.

Halaa': Having the ability to deal successfully with the "spirit" or "immaterial" world. See Chapter 9.

Jah: (1) In West Semai, having lost one's *halaa'* ability. (2) In some other Senoi languages, "person," for example, *Jah Hut, Jakun.*

Kəloog: A formless entity that maintains life; will, vitality, consciousness. See Chapter 9.

Kətmoid: A *nyani'* associated with death and graves. See Chapter 9.

Mai: (1) They-more-than-two. (2) People who have certain characteristics, for example, *Mai Biuug* or *Mai Biyeg,* "Pale People" (Europeans) or *Mai Darat,* "Hinterland People" (aborigines). (3) Other people; hence (4) Outgroupers: people toward whom one has few obligations, if any, and in whose affairs one has little or no interest. The term is used differently in different contexts, for example, nonkinsman, person from another *gu,* non-Semai. The connotation seems to be "unreliable, probably dangerous, and partly incomprehensible person."

Mənai: From *mai* (q.v.) + infix *-ən-*. Spouse's younger sibling or elder sibling's spouse. East Semai *mənai* can engage in joking, horseplay, and sexual intimacies with each other. See Chapter 8.

Naga, Dangga': From Sanskrit, by way of Malay *naga.* A huge, black, subterranean, snakelike, horned dragon. In some ways the epitome of reptiles, for example, the "subterraneans"—python, crocodile, giant monitor lizard—are its "adopted children." Cf. Semelai *naga',* described as a huge cobra with "soft horns"; and Malay *naga, balun bidai.*

Nyani', jani': ?From *nya'ni',* "pain." Entity used to explain pain when there is no empirically observable agent causing the pain. In some contexts, an abstraction, like "disease"; in others, more personalized, like "evil spirit"; in yet others, quite concrete, like "evil supernatural beast," for example, certain species of animals are *nyani'.* Cf. Jah Hut *bes.* See Chapter 9.

Panali': From Malay *pemali* or *pali,* "taboo at all times" + infix *-ən-*. (1) An action taboo at all times. (2) The calamity said to follow such an action. (3) More strictly, mixing together types of food that should be kept separate; and the calamity such mixing produces. See Chapter 3.

Pərsusah: From *pər-,* causative prefix + Malay *susah,* "difficult, distressing." Broadly, to put someone into an unpleasant emotional state, for example, irritation, annoyance. More concretely, to interfere in someone's affairs without being asked or to make difficulties for him; to bother someone. The closest English equivalent is the colloquial verb "bug." Not as serious as *punan* (q.v.) but can lead to *punan.* See Chapter 6.

Punan, pəhunan: From Malay *kĕmpunan,* which has the same root as English "taboo." (1) A frustrated desire that makes one sick or accident prone. (2) An action which produces such a mental condition, for example, hurting someone's feelings. (3) The rule against committing such actions. (4) More generally, taboo at all times. (5) The sickness or accident-proneness resulting from *punan* acts. See Chapter 6.

Ruai: A small entity normally located just behind the forehead; occurs in human beings, certain individual animals, and (say the west Semai) in one's rice crop. Its three sets of characteristics serve to account for certain experiences. First, it is a miniature replica of the body it inhabits; hence, the sense of personal identity in dreams, which are the experiences of one's wandering *ruai.* Second, it is a bird, for one often dreams of people and places too far away to be reached except by flying. Finally it is a timid child, easily frightened away, as demonstrated by the skittish behavior of *gunig* (q.v.) and by the occurrence of *ruai* loss in children who have been frightened. (The notion of a "rice soul" is a modification of a Malay belief. The concept of the soul as a bird is common in Southeast Asia.) See Chapter 9.

Sumbung: ?From Malay *sombong,* "arrogant, self-assertive" + Malay *sumbang,* "incest." Acting or feeling as if one was better than other people; more specifically in the case of youngsters, irreverence for or behaving disrespectfully toward one's elders; being too intimate with one's elders, thus increasing the danger of incest. See Chapter 6.

Tərlaid: From *?təlaid* + causative infix *-r-*. (1) Performing an action (for example, incest) that invites a natural calamity (for example, thundersquall, flood, yaws). (2) The calamity itself. (The complex of beliefs associated with this concept is most highly developed in the east, where people are in contact with Semang. Grammatically, the word for the calamity should be *təlaid,* although most Semai do not know this word. But *cf.* Báteq Semang *təlaid.*) See Chapter 2.

Recommended Reading

CAREY, I. Y., 1961. *Tengleq Kui Serok*. Kuala Lumpur, Malaysia: Dewan Bahasa dan Pustaka.
A study, written in English, of the Temiar language, including a useful 60 page summary of the ethnography of these Senoi-speaking northern neighbors of the Semai.

GULLICK, J. M., 1958, *Indigenous Political Systems of Western Malaya*. London School of Economics Monographs on Social Anthropology, No. 17.
A description of Malay society before British influence became dominant. The chapter on the Malay village community suggests interesting comparisons with the Semai.

HODDER, B. W., 1959, *Man in Malaya*. London: University of London Press, Ltd.
A short, interesting study of the cultural and biological adaptations of a wide variety of peoples to the physical environment of Malaya.

LEACH, E. R., 1965, *Political Systems of Highland Burma*. Boston: The Beacon Press.
A paperback reprint of the classic 1954 study of a Southeast Asian hill people whose society, although organized along completely different lines, affords the same sort of leeway for individual maneuvering that Semai society does.

LEBAR, F. M., G. C. HICKEY, and J. K. MUSGRAVE (eds.) 1964. *Ethnic Groups of Mainland Southeast Asia*. New Haven, Conn.: Human Relations Area Files Press.
A useful collection of ethnographic summaries on the entire area, with extensive bibliographies.

NOONE, H. D., 1936, *Report on the Settlements and Welfare of the Ple-Temiar Senoi of the Perak-Kelatan Watershed*. Journal of the Federated Malay States Museums, Vol. 19, Part 1.
The first extensive report on a Senoi people by a trained anthropologist.

SKEAT, W. W., and C. O. BLAGDEN, 1906, *Pagan Races of the Malay Peninsula*. London: Macmillan & Co., Ltd.
A massive compendium of all the then available material on the Malayan aborigines. It is sometimes hard to tell which references refer to which Malayan people.

WILLIAMS-HUNT, P. D. R., 1952, *An Introduction to the Malayan Aborigines.* Kuala
Lumpur, Malaysia: Government Press.
A chatty but informative account for the general reader by a gifted amateur whom
the west Semai still remember with affection. Includes an extensive annotated
bibliography and a list of the museums in Britain, Australia, and Malaysia that
contain Semai and other aboriginal collections.

Collections of Semai Materials in the United States and France

American Museum of Natural History (New York City)
Materials and photographs collected in the 1960s by the author and extensively documented. Also in this museum is a large collection of carvings by the Jah Hut Senoi.

Field Museum of Natural History (Chicago)
Two collections, one made in the 1920s by Fay-Cooper Cole and catalogued as "Central
Sakai." The documentation is not extensive, but there are some good photographs
which can be ordered from the museum. Some of Cole's collection is on display. The
other collection, made by R. Martin around the turn of the century, is of uncertain
provenience and undocumented except for the collector's suggestion that one read his
book, *Die Inlandstämme der Malayischen Halbinsel* (Jena, 1905).

Musée d'Homme (Paris)
Materials of sometimes uncertain provenience, mostly Semai and mostly collected by
the talented amateur Louis Carrard in the 1930s and cataloged as "Sakai." Includes
excellent photographs.